Classic Baking

Classic Baking

AS GOOD TODAY AS IT WAS THEN!

This edition published by Parragon Books Ltd in 2013
LOVE FOOD is an imprint of Parragon Books Ltd

Parragon Books Ltd
Chartist House
15–17 Trim Street
Bath BA1 1HA, UK
www.parragon.com/lovefood

ISBN: 978-1-4723-2914-1

Printed in China

Designed by Sabine Vonderstein
New recipes by Angela Drake
Edited by Lin Thomas and Angela Drake

Notes for the Reader
This book uses both metric and imperial measurements. Follow the same units of measurement throughout; do not mix metric and imperial. All spoon measurements are level: teaspoons are assumed to be 5 ml, and tablespoons are assumed to be 15 ml. Unless otherwise stated, milk is assumed to be full fat, eggs and individual vegetables are medium, and pepper is freshly ground black pepper. Unless otherwise stated, all root vegetables should be washed in plain water and peeled prior to using.

Garnishes, decorations and serving suggestions are all optional and not necessarily included in the recipe ingredients or method. The times given are an approximate guide only. Preparation times differ according to the techniques used by different people and the cooking times may also vary from those given. Optional ingredients, variations or serving suggestions have not been included in the time calculations.

Recipes using raw or very lightly cooked eggs should be avoided by infants, the elderly, pregnant women, convalescents and anyone suffering from an illness. Pregnant and breastfeeding women are advised to avoid eating peanuts and peanut products. Sufferers from nut allergies should be aware that some of the ready-made ingredients used in the recipes in this book may contain nuts. Always check the packaging before use. Vegetarians should be aware that some of the ready-made ingredients used in the recipes in this book may contain animal products. Always check the packaging before use.

Picture acknowledgements
The publisher would like to thank the following for permission to reproduce copyright material:

Getty Images: cover Sally Williams Photography; p.10 Alison Gootee; p.44 bottom image Shawna Lemay; p.45 and 146 top image Sharon Lapkin; p.115 top image Foodcollection RF; p.124 Ideas/Ed O'Riley; p. 145 and p.222 Studer-T. Veronika; p.147 Crystal Cartier; p.156 Anna Nemoy (Xaomena); p.172 top left image MargoLuc; p.173 Nichola Evans; p.182 top image Susie Adams; p.208 Michael Paul; p.223 Alexandra Grablewski; p.242 bottom right Karin Enge Vivar; p.243 Jill Ferry
iStock: additional images, ornaments and background note paper: p.2, 8, 9, 11, 36, 68, 72, 114, p.182 bottom right Emilie Duchesne, p.183 Svetlana Kolpakova
Sabine Vonderstein: flower images and postcard images; p.115 bottom right image; p.146 bottom right image; p.242 left images
Lace backgrounds: from the publication 'Lace', published by The Pepin Press, www.pepinpress.com

Contents

Introduction

Few types of cookery are more satisfying than baking, and it's a tradition worth keeping in every home. While shop-bought cakes are perfectly proportioned and immaculately presented there's nothing like the smell of a gorgeous cake baking in the oven. The flavour will almost certainly be far superior and you'll also know exactly what went into it!

Home baking has never been so popular and the trend for all things vintage has made us want to reach for our grandmothers' cookbooks for the classic recipes. With a wide variety of recipes to choose from, Classic Baking is intended to contain those traditional recipes that your grandmother made, from the timeless Chocolate Cake, Lemon Drizzle Loaf and Carrot Cake to delicious Summer Fruit Tartlets, Chocolate Chip Cookies and Vanilla Cupcakes.

The basic skills of baking are very easy to learn and you need very little in the way of special equipment to make some impressive cakes and other baked goods. There are a few tips that are worth noting to ensure success. Before you start, always preheat the oven to the correct temperature so it is ready to use once your cake is mixed. Read through the recipe, assemble all your ingredients and measure everything before you start. Resist the temptation to open the oven door too often, and close it gently rather than banging it shut. Always make sure your cake is completely cool before storing.

Most importantly, remember that baking is a fun and rewarding pastime. The cakes and bakes you make will be individual because they were made by you. So, why not revive the tradition of baking in your home today? You'll never be short of a home-baked treat to offer visitors when they drop by! All it needs is a little practice and you'll soon be turning out impressive cakes and baked goods for all the family to enjoy.

Happy Baking!

Traybakes

Almond Butter Cake

Serves 15

Ingredients

350 g/12 oz strong plain white
  flour, plus extra for dusting
7 g sachet easy-bake dried yeast
25 g/1 oz caster sugar
pinch of salt
125 ml/4 fl oz milk
55 g/2 oz lightly salted butter,
  diced, plus extra for greasing
2 large eggs, lightly beaten

For the Topping

175 g/6 oz unsalted butter,
  softened
70 g/2 ½ oz flaked almonds
55 g/2 oz caster sugar
¼ tsp ground cinnamon

1. Grease a 23-cm x 33-cm/9-inch x 13-inch Swiss roll tin. Place the flour in a large bowl and stir in the dried yeast, sugar and salt. Make a well in the centre.

2. Place the milk and butter in a small saucepan and heat gently until the butter has melted. Leave to cool for a few minutes until the liquid is hand hot.

3. Pour the milk mixture and beaten eggs into the bowl and mix well with round-bladed knife to make a soft, sticky dough. Turn the dough onto a lightly floured surface and knead for 7–8 minutes until smooth and elastic, adding a little more flour if the dough is sticky.

4. Roll the dough out to a rectangle almost as large as the prepared tin. Place the dough in the tin and push into the corners with your finger tips. Cover with lightly greased clingfilm and leave in a warm place for 45–55 minutes, or until the dough is puffy and has risen above the edges of the tin. Preheat the oven to 200°C/400°F/ Gas Mark 6.

5. For the topping, place the butter in a bowl and beat until very pale and fluffy. Spoon into a piping bag fitted with a small plain nozzle.

6. Using two fingers make deep indentations into the risen dough at even intervals (approximately two finger widths apart). Pipe the butter into the indentations. Scatter over the flaked almonds. Mix together the sugar and cinnamon and sprinkle over the almonds.

7. Bake in the preheated oven for 12–15 minutes, then cover loosely with foil and bake for a further 5–8 minutes, or until the cake is springy to the touch with a golden brown topping. Leave in the tin for 10 minutes, then cut into slices. Serve warm or cold.

Coconut Bars

1. Preheat the oven to 180°C/350°F/Gas Mark 4. Grease a 23-cm/9-inch square cake tin and line the base with non-stick baking paper.

2. Cream together the butter and caster sugar until pale and fluffy, then gradually beat in the eggs. Stir in the orange rind, orange juice and soured cream. Fold in the flour and desiccated coconut evenly using a metal spoon.

3. Spoon the mixture into the prepared cake tin and level the surface. Bake in the preheated oven for 35–40 minutes, or until risen and firm to the touch.

4. Leave to cool for 10 minutes in the tin, then turn out and finish cooling on a wire rack.

5. For the frosting, lightly beat the egg white, and stir in the icing sugar and desiccated coconut, adding enough orange juice to mix to a thick paste. Spread over the top of the cake, sprinkle with toasted shredded coconut, then leave to set before slicing into bars.

Makes 10

Ingredients
125 g/4½ oz unsalted butter,
  plus extra for greasing
225 g/8 oz golden caster sugar
2 eggs, beaten
finely grated rind of 1 orange
3 tbsp orange juice
150 ml/5 fl oz soured cream
140 g/5 oz self-raising flour
85 g/3 oz desiccated coconut
toasted shredded coconut,
  to decorate

For the Frosting
1 egg white
200 g/7 oz icing sugar
85 g/3 oz desiccated coconut
about 1 tbsp orange juice

Poppy Seed Streusel

Serves 12

Ingredients

225 g/8 oz self-raising flour
175 g/6 oz caster sugar
3 eggs, lightly beaten
finely grated zest of ½ lemon
100 ml/3½ fl oz sunflower oil
3 tbsp milk
50 g/1¾ oz poppy seeds

For the Streusel Topping

115 g/4 oz plain flour
70 g/2½ oz butter, at room
  temperature, diced, plus extra
  for greasing
85 g/3 oz caster sugar
icing sugar, for dusting

1. Preheat the oven to 170°C/325°F/Gas Mark 3. Grease a 23-cm x 33-cm/9-inch x 13-inch Swiss roll tin.

2. Sift the flour into a large bowl. Add the sugar, eggs, lemon zest, oil and milk. Using an electric hand-held whisk beat together until thoroughly combined. Stir in the poppy seeds.

3. Spoon the mixture into the prepared tin and gently spread out to the edges of the tin using a spatula.

4. To make the streusel topping, place the flour and butter in a bowl. Using your fingertips, rub the butter into the flour until the mixture resembles fine breadcrumbs. Stir in the sugar. Spoon the streusel over the cake mixture in an even layer, pressing down gently.

5. Bake in the preheated oven for 45–50 minutes, or until the top is light golden and a skewer inserted into the cake comes out clean.

6. Leave to cool in the tin for 20 minutes then transfer to a wire rack and leave to cool completely. Dust with icing sugar and cut into squares to serve.

Poppy Seed Crumble Squares

1. Grease an 18-cm x 28-cm/7-inch x 11-inch traybake tin. Place the flour in a large bowl and stir in the dried yeast and sugar. Make a well in the centre. Place the milk and butter in a small saucepan and heat gently until the butter has melted. Leave to cool for a few minutes until the liquid is hand hot.

2. Pour the milk mixture and beaten egg into the bowl and mix well with round-bladed knife to make a soft, sticky dough. Turn the dough onto a lightly floured surface and knead for 5–6 minutes until smooth and elastic, adding a little more flour if the dough is sticky. Roll the dough out to a rectangle almost as large as the prepared tin. Place the dough in the tin and push into the corners with your fingertips. Cover with lightly greased clingfilm and leave in a warm place for 1 hour 30 minutes, or until the dough is puffy and has almost doubled in size.

3. About 30 minutes before the dough is ready make the filling. Mix the cornflour and 4 tbsp of the milk in a heatproof bowl. Place the rest of the milk in a saucepan with the poppy seeds and sugar. Slowly bring to the boil then whisk into the cornflour mixture. Return the mixture to the saucepan and heat gently, stirring all the time until smooth and thick. Transfer to a bowl, stir in the raisins and lemon zest and leave to cool for 20 minutes, stirring frequently to prevent a skin forming. Preheat the oven to 180°C/350°F/ Gas Mark 4. Gently spread the poppy seed mixture in an even layer over the risen dough.

4. To make the crumble, place the flour in a bowl and add the diced butter. Rub into the flour until the mixture resembles large breadcrumbs. Stir in the sugar. Sprinkle over the poppy seed filling. Bake in the preheated oven for 30–35 minutes, or until the topping is golden. Leave in the tin for 20 minutes then transfer to a wire rack and leave to cool completely before slicing.

Makes 12

Ingredients
200 g/7 oz strong white plain
    flour, plus extra for dusting
1 tsp easy-bake dried yeast
40 g/1½ oz caster sugar
5 tbsp milk
25 g/1 oz butter, plus extra
    for greasing
1 egg, lightly beaten

For the Filling
3 tbsp cornflour
300 ml/10 fl oz milk
55 g/2 oz poppy seeds
100 g/3½ oz caster sugar
40 g/1½ oz raisins
finely grated zest of ½ lemon

For the Crumble
70 g/2½ oz self-raising flour
50 g/1¾ oz butter, at room
    temperature, diced
40 g/1½ oz caster sugar

Classic Crumble Bars

Makes 8

Ingredients
225 g/8 oz strong plain flour,
    plus extra for dusting
1½ tsp easy-bake dried yeast
55 g/2 oz caster sugar
2 tsp finely grated lemon zest
150 ml/5 fl oz milk
85 g/3 oz butter, plus extra
    for greasing

For the Crumble
150 g/5½ oz plain flour
70 g/2 ½ oz butter,
    at room temperature, diced
70 g/2½ oz caster sugar
icing sugar, for dusting

1. Grease an 18-cm x 28-cm/7-inch x 11-inch traybake tin. Place the flour in a large bowl and stir in the dried yeast, sugar and lemon zest. Make a well in the centre.

2. Place the milk and 70 g/2½ oz of the butter in a small saucepan and heat gently until the butter has melted. Leave to cool for a few minutes until the liquid is hand hot.

3. Pour the milk mixture into the bowl and mix well with a round-bladed knife to make a soft, sticky dough. Turn the dough onto a lightly floured surface and knead for 7–8 minutes until smooth and elastic, adding a little more flour if the dough is sticky.

4. Place the dough in a clean bowl. Cover with greased clingfilm and leave in a warm place for 1–1¼ hours, or until the dough has almost doubled in size.

5. Turn the dough onto a lightly floured surface and re-knead for 1 minute. Roll out to a rectangle almost as large as the prepared tin. Place the dough in the tin and push it into the corners with your fingertips. Cover with greased clingfilm and leave in a warm place for 25–30 minutes, or until the dough is puffy. Preheat the oven to 180°C/350°F/Gas Mark 4.

6. To make the crumble, place the flour in a bowl and add the diced butter. Rub into the flour until the mixture resembles large breadcrumbs. Stir in the sugar.

7. Melt the remaining butter and brush lightly all over the risen dough. Top with the crumble mixture. Bake in the preheated oven for 40–45 minutes, or until the crumble topping is golden brown. Leave in the tin for 10 minutes then transfer to a wire rack. Serve warm or cold cut into bars and dusted with icing sugar.

Chocolate Crumble Squares

1. Grease a 28-cm x 18-cm/11-inch x 7-inch traybake tin and line the base with baking paper.

2. To make the custard, blend the custard powder and sugar with 2 tbsp of the milk in a small heatproof bowl until smooth. Heat the rest of the milk in a small pan until almost boiling then whisk into the custard mixture.

3. Pour the mixture back into the pan and slowly bring to the boil, stirring all the time, to make a smooth and thick custard. Pour the custard into a clean bowl, cover the surface with a sheet of baking paper (to prevent a skin forming) and leave until cold. Preheat the oven to 180°C/350°F/Gas Mark 4.

4. To make the chocolate sponge, place all the ingredients in a large bowl and, using an electric hand-held whisk, beat together until smooth and creamy.

5. Spoon the mixture into the prepared tin and gently level the surface with a spatula. Using a teaspoon, drop small dollops of custard all over the top of the chocolate sponge mixture. Use a knife to gently swirl the custard through the chocolate sponge mixture.

6. To make the crumble, place the flour and butter in a bowl and using your fingertips, rub the butter into the flour to resemble coarse breadcrumbs. Stir in the sugar and scatter the crumble over the top of the cake.

7. Bake in the preheated oven for 30–35 minutes, or until risen, golden and a skewer inserted into the cake comes out clean. Leave to cool completely in the tin, then dust with icing sugar and cut into squares to serve.

Makes 12

Ingredients
1½ tbsp custard powder
1½ tbsp caster sugar
200 ml/7 fl oz milk

For the Chocolate Sponge
175 g/6 oz butter, softened, plus extra for greasing
150 g/5 ½ oz caster sugar
3 eggs
150 g/5 ½ oz self-raising flour, sifted
25 g/1 oz cocoa powder, sifted

For the Crumble
50 g/1¾ oz self-raising flour
40 g/1½ oz butter, at room temperature, diced
1½ tbsp caster sugar
icing sugar, for dusting

Chocolate & Cherry Cream Slices

Makes 20

Ingredients
175 g/6 oz self-raising flour
½ tsp baking powder
175 g/6 oz butter, softened,
  plus extra for greasing
175 g/6 oz caster sugar
1 tsp vanilla extract
3 eggs, lightly beaten
3 tbsp milk
1 ½ tbsp cocoa powder
350 g/12 oz frozen pitted
  black cherries, defrosted
  and thoroughly drained

For the Filling
3 leaves of gelatine
6 tbsp water
200 g/7 oz medium-fat
  soft cheese
40 g/1½ oz caster sugar
350 ml/12 fl oz double cream,
  softly whipped

For the Chocolate Glaze
150 g/5 ½ oz dark chocolate,
  broken into pieces
25 g/1 oz unsalted butter
2 tsp golden syrup

1. Preheat the oven to 180°C/350°F/Gas Mark 4. Grease a 33-cm x 23-cm/13-inch x 9-inch traybake tin (about 5 cm/2 inches deep) and line the base and sides with baking paper (making sure the paper comes about 1 cm/½ inch above the edges of the tin).

2. Sift the self-raising flour and baking powder into a large bowl. Add the butter, sugar, vanilla extract, eggs and one tablespoon of the milk. Using a hand-held electric mixer beat together for 2–3 minutes until the mixture is thoroughly combined. Spoon half the mixture into the prepared tin and gently level the surface with a spatula. Beat the remaining milk and cocoa powder into the rest of the mixture and spread evenly over the top. Draw a knife through the two mixtures to create a swirled effect. Scatter over the cherries. Bake in the preheated oven for 30–35 minutes, or until just firm to the touch and a skewer inserted into the cake comes out clean. Leave to cool completely in the tin.

3. To make the filling, place the gelatine leaves and water in a small saucepan and leave to soak for 10 minutes. Heat very gently, stirring all the time, until the gelatine has completely dissolved. Leave to cool for 20 minutes. Place the soft cheese and sugar in a bowl and beat together until smooth. Fold in the softly whipped cream then fold in the cooled gelatine liquid. Spread over the top of the sponge cake, levelling the surface with a palette knife. Chill in the fridge for 2 hours, or until the filling is set.

4. To make the chocolate glaze, place the chocolate, butter and syrup in a heatproof bowl set over a pan of simmering water and leave until melted. Remove from the heat and stir until smooth. Leave the glaze for about 20 minutes, stirring occasionally until cooled but still spreadable. Using the paper as a guide lift the cake out of the tin and place on a board. Using a warmed palette knife, quickly spread the chocolate glaze in a thin and even layer over the filling. Use the prongs of a fork to draw wavy lines on the chocolate and cut into slices before the glaze sets.

Plum Crumble Slices

1. Preheat the oven to 180°C/350°F/Gas Mark 4. Grease a 28-cm x 18-cm/11-inch x 7-inch traybake tin and line the base with baking paper.

2. Place the butter, sugar and almond extract in a large bowl and, using a hand-held electric whisk, beat together until pale and creamy. Gradually beat in the eggs.

3. Sift over the flour and fold into the mixture with the ground almonds until thoroughly combined. Spread the mixture in an even layer in the prepared tin.

4. Arrange the plum quarters over the top of the sponge mixture, cut side facing up, pressing them down gently.

5. To make the crumble topping, place the flour and butter in a bowl and rub the butter into the flour until the mixture resembles coarse breadcrumbs. Stir in the sugar.

6. Scatter the crumble mixture over the plums. Bake in the preheated oven for 40–50 minutes, or until a skewer inserted into the cake comes out clean. Cover loosely with foil after 35 minutes to prevent the top over-browning.

7. Leave the cake to cool in the tin for 20 minutes, then transfer to a wire rack. Serve warm or cold, dusted with icing sugar and cut into squares.

Makes 12

Ingredients
115 g/4 oz butter, softened,
  plus extra for greasing
115 g/4 oz caster sugar
½ tsp almond extract
2 large eggs, lightly beaten
115 g/4 oz self-raising flour
25 g/1 oz ground almonds
450 g/1 lb plums, halved,
  stoned removed and
  quartered

For the Crumble
70 g/2 ½ oz self-raising flour
40 g/1 ½ oz butter, at room
  temperature, diced
25 g/1 oz caster sugar
icing sugar, for dusting

Plum Squares

Makes 15

Ingredients

350 g/12 oz self-raising flour,
  plus extra for dusting
225 g/8 oz butter, at room
  temperature, diced, plus extra
  for greasing
150 g/5½ oz caster sugar
2 eggs, lightly beaten
finely grated zest ½ lemon

For the Topping

150 g/5½ oz medium-fat
  soft cheese
1 egg, lightly beaten
25 g/1 oz caster sugar
1 tbsp cornflour
5 tbsp plum or damson jam
icing sugar, for dusting

1. Grease a 23-cm x33-cm/9-inch x 13-inch Swiss roll tin and line the base with baking paper. Preheat the oven to 180°C/350°F/ Gas Mark 4.

2. Sift the flour into a large bowl and add the diced butter. Rub the butter into the flour until the mixture resembles coarse breadcrumbs then stir in the sugar. Remove 125 g/4½ oz of the crumble mixture and set aside in a bowl.

3. Stir the beaten eggs and lemon zest into the remaining crumble mixture and mix with a round-bladed knife until beginning to clump together. Gather into a soft dough with your hands. Press the dough into the base of the prepared tin, using the palms of your hands (dusted with a little flour if the mixture is too sticky).

4. To make the topping, place the soft cheese in a bowl and gradually beat in the egg, sugar and cornflour until smooth. Spread over the base.

5. Drop small spoonfuls of the jam all over the soft cheese mixture then top with the reserved crumble.

6. Bake in the preheated oven for 35–40 minutes, or until just golden and set. Leave to cool in the tin for 20 minutes then transfer to a wire rack to cool completely. Dust with icing sugar then cut into squares to serve.

Apple Strudels

1. Preheat the oven to 200°C/400°F/Gas Mark 6. Lightly butter a large baking tray.

2. To make the filling, place the raisins in a small bowl and add the hot rum or apple juice. Leave to soak for 15 minutes.

3. Place the apple slices in a large bowl and toss in the lemon juice and vanilla extract. Add the sugar, cinnamon, flaked almonds and soaked raisins and mix together gently.

4. In a separate bowl beat together the soft cheese with half the cream and the egg yolks until smooth. Add the apple mixture to this bowl and stir gently to mix.

5. Take one sheet of the filo pastry and brush lightly with melted butter then sprinkle with some of the breadcrumbs. Spoon one sixth of the apple filling on to the lower third of the sheet. Gently roll up the pastry to enclose the filling and pinch both the pastry ends together tightly.

6. Place, join-side down, on the prepared baking sheet and repeat with the rest of the sheets of filo pastry and filling to make six strudels in total. Brush the top of the strudels with the rest of the cream. Bake in the preheated oven for 25–30 minutes until light golden. Serve warm, dusted with icing sugar.

Makes 6

Ingredients
3 tbsp raisins
1 tbsp hot rum or apple juice
6 small dessert apples, peeled, cored and thinly sliced
1 tbsp lemon juice
1 tsp vanilla extract
100 g/3 ½ oz caster sugar
½ tsp ground cinnamon
3 tbsp flaked almonds, lightly toasted
100 g/3 ½ oz medium-fat soft cheese or Quark
4 tbsp single cream
2 egg yolks
6 sheets filo pastry, each about 20 cm x 30 cm (8 inch x 12 inch)
40 g/1½ oz butter, melted, plus extra for greasing
3 tbsp fresh white breadcrumbs
icing sugar, for dusting

Chocolate & Cinnamon Brownies

Makes 16

Ingredients
115 g/4 oz plain chocolate,
* broken into pieces*
200 g/7 oz butter, plus extra
* for greasing*
85 g/3 oz pecan nut halves
250 g/9 oz caster sugar
4 eggs, beaten
225 g/8 oz plain flour
2 tsp ground cinnamon
55 g/2 oz white chocolate,
* broken into pieces*
2 tbsp milk
115 g/4 oz icing sugar

1. Preheat the oven to 180°C/350°F/Gas Mark 4. Grease a 23-cm/9-inch shallow square cake tin.

2. Melt the plain chocolate and 175 g/6 oz of the butter in a heatproof bowl, set over a saucepan of gently simmering water. Remove from the heat and allow to cool slightly.

3. Set 16 pecan halves to one side for decoration and chop the rest. Beat together the caster sugar and eggs with a whisk until thick and creamy. Then fold in the chocolate mixture, flour, cinnamon and chopped pecans.

4. Transfer the mixture to the prepared tin and bake in the preheated oven for 35–40 minutes, or until just firm to the touch. Leave to cool in the tin.

5. Melt the remaining butter and white chocolate in a heatproof bowl, set over a saucepan of gently simmering water. Remove from the heat and beat in the milk and icing sugar. Spread this mixture over the cooled brownies. Allow to set for 30 minutes then cut into 16 squares and top each square with a pecan half.

Fudge Blondies

1. Preheat the oven to 180°C/350°F/Gas Mark 4. Grease a 20-cm/8-inch shallow square cake tin and line with baking paper.

2. Place the butter and brown sugar in a large bowl and whisk together until pale and creamy. Gradually whisk in the eggs and vanilla extract. Sift the flour and baking powder into the mixture and beat together until well mixed.

3. Add the fudge and chopped nuts and stir together until combined. Spoon the mixture into the prepared tin and smooth the surface.

4. Bake in the preheated oven for 40–45 minutes, or until risen and golden brown. Leave to cool in the tin, then dust with sifted icing sugar to decorate, and cut into squares.

Makes 9

Ingredients

125 g/4½ oz butter, softened, plus extra for greasing
200 g/7 oz soft light brown sugar
2 large eggs, beaten
1 tsp vanilla extract
250 g/9 oz plain flour
1 tsp baking powder
125 g/4½ oz soft butter fudge, chopped into small pieces
70 g/2½ oz macadamia nuts, roughly chopped
icing sugar, for dusting

Double Chocolate Pecan Blondies

Makes 12

Ingredients

- 250 g/9 oz white chocolate, broken into pieces
- 40 g/1½ oz butter, plus extra for greasing
- 175 g/6 oz plain chocolate
- 2 large eggs, beaten
- 85 g/3 oz caster sugar
- 115 g/4 oz self-raising flour
- 100 g/3½ oz pecan nuts, roughly chopped

1. Preheat the oven to 180°C/350°F/Gas Mark 4. Grease a 20-cm/8-inch shallow square baking tin and line with baking paper.

2. Place 85 g/3 oz of the white chocolate in a heatproof bowl and add the butter. Set the bowl over a saucepan of gently simmering water and heat, stirring occasionally, until melted and smooth. Meanwhile, roughly chop the remaining white and plain chocolate.

3. Beat the eggs and sugar together in a large bowl then stir in the melted chocolate mixture. Sift the flour over the top. Add the chopped chocolate and pecan nuts. Mix well.

4. Spoon the mixture into the prepared tin and smooth the surface. Bake in the preheated oven for 35–40 minutes, or until golden brown and just firm to the touch in the centre. Leave in the tin until completely cooled and the chocolate chunks inside have set, then turn out and cut into pieces.

Chocolate & Cherry Brownies

Makes 12

Ingredients

- 175 g/6 oz plain chocolate, broken into pieces
- 175 g/6 oz butter, plus extra for greasing
- 225 g/8 oz caster sugar
- 3 large eggs, beaten
- 1 tsp vanilla extract
- 125 g/4½ oz self-raising flour
- 175 g/6 oz fresh cherries, stoned
- 85 g/3 oz white chocolate

1. Preheat the oven to 180°C/350°F/Gas Mark 4. Grease a 24-cm x 20-cm/9½ x 8-inch shallow cake tin and line with baking paper.

2. Put the plain chocolate and butter into a large, heatproof bowl set over a saucepan of simmering water and heat until melted. Remove from the heat and leave to cool for 5 minutes.

3. Beat the sugar, eggs and vanilla extract into the chocolate mixture. Sift in the flour and fold in gently. Pour the mixture into the prepared tin. Scatter over the cherries. Chop the white chocolate and scatter over the top.

4. Bake in the preheated oven for 30 minutes. Loosely cover the tops of the brownies with foil and bake for a further 15–20 minutes, or until just firm to the touch. Leave to cool in the tin, then cut into pieces.

Apple Crumble Squares

Makes 15

Ingredients
175 g/6 oz butter, softened,
    plus extra for greasing
125 g/4 ½ oz caster sugar
1 tsp vanilla extract
2 large eggs, lightly beaten
175 g/6 oz self-raising flour
3 tbsp milk
finely grated zest of ½ lemon
500 g/1 lb 2 oz dessert apples,
    peeled, cored and thinly
sliced
1 tbsp lemon juice

For the Crumble Topping
115 g/4 oz self-raising flour
85 g/3 oz butter
55 g/2 oz caster sugar
25 g/1 oz ground almonds
icing sugar, for dusting

1. Preheat the oven to 170°C/325°F/Gas Mark 3. Grease a 33-cm x 23-cm/13-inch x 9-inch tray bake tin (about 5-cm/2-inches deep) and line the base with baking paper.

2. Place the butter, sugar and vanilla extract in a large bowl and, using a hand-held electric whisk, beat together until pale and creamy. Gradually beat in the eggs.

3. Sift over the flour and fold into the mixture with the milk and lemon zest until thoroughly combined. Spread the mixture in an even layer in the prepared tin.

4. Toss the apples in the lemon juice and arrange over the top of the sponge mixture.

5. To make the crumble topping, place the flour and butter in a bowl and rub the butter into the flour until the mixture resembles coarse breadcrumbs. Stir in the sugar and ground almonds.

6. Scatter the crumble mixture over the apples. Bake in the preheated oven for 45–50 minutes, or until the topping is golden and a skewer inserted into the cake comes out clean.

7. Leave the cake to cool in the tin. Serve warm or cold, dusted with icing sugar and cut into squares.

Pear Squares

1. Preheat the oven to 180°C/350°F/Gas Mark 4. Grease a 28-cm x 18-cm/11-inch x 7-inch traybake tin and line the base with baking paper.

2. Place the butter, sugar, vanilla extract and lemon zest in a large bowl and, using an electric hand-held whisk, beat together until pale and creamy. Gradually beat in the eggs. Sift over the flour and fold into the mixture with the milk.

3. Spoon the mixture into the prepared tin and gently level the surface with a spatula. Arrange the sliced pears on top of the sponge mixture, pressing them down gently. Scatter over the raisins and almonds.

4. Bake in the preheated oven for 45–50 minutes, or until risen, golden and firm to the touch.

5. Brush the top of the hot cake liberally with the warmed and sieved apricot jam. Leave the cake to cool in the tin for 20 minutes then transfer to a wire rack to cool completely. Dust with icing sugar, then cut into squares to serve.

Makes 15

Ingredients
225 g/8 oz butter, softened,
*   plus extra for greasing*
225 g/8 oz caster sugar
1 tsp vanilla extract
finely grated zest of ½ lemon
4 eggs, lightly beaten
225 g/8 oz self-raising flour
3 tbsp milk
3 small pears (approx 350 g/
*   12 oz in total) peeled,*
*   cored and sliced*
2 tbsp raisins
2 tbsp flaked almonds
2 tbsp apricot jam,
*   warmed and sieved*
icing sugar, for dusting

Chocolate & Pear Squares

Makes 20

Ingredients

175 g/6 oz self-raising flour
2 tbsp cocoa powder
½ tsp baking powder
175 g/6 oz butter, softened,
 plus extra for greasing
175 g/6 oz caster sugar
1 tsp vanilla extract
3 eggs
55 g/2 oz dark chocolate,
 melted
410 g can pear halves in
 natural juice, drained
 reserving 100 ml/3 ½ fl oz
 of the juice

For the Topping

3 leaves of gelatine
400 ml/14 fl oz double cream
4 tbsp icing sugar, sifted
300 ml/10 fl oz soured cream

To Decorate

1 tbsp icing sugar
1 tbsp cocoa powder

1. Preheat the oven to 180°C/350°F/Gas Mark 4. Grease a 33-cm x 23-cm/13-inch x 9-inch traybake tin (about 5-cm/2-inches deep) and line the base and sides with baking paper (making sure the paper comes about 1 cm/½ inch above the edges of the tin).

2. Sift the self-raising flour, cocoa and baking powder into a large bowl. Add the butter, sugar, vanilla extract and eggs. Using a hand-held electric mixer beat together for 2–3 minutes until the mixture is thoroughly combined. Fold in the melted chocolate. Spoon the mixture into the prepared tin and gently level the surface with a spatula. Thinly slice the drained pear halves and arrange over the chocolate sponge, pressing down gently.

3. Bake in the preheated oven for 30–35 minutes, or until just firm to the touch and a skewer inserted into the cake comes out clean. Leave to cool completely in the tin. To make the topping, place the gelatine leaves in a shallow bowl and cover with cold water. Leave to soak for 5 minutes until soft. Remove the leaves from the water and squeeze out the excess liquid. Place the leaves in a small pan with the reserved pear juice. Heat gently until the gelatine has completely dissolved. Leave to cool for 15 minutes.

4. Whip the cream and icing sugar together in a large bowl until holding firm peaks. Fold in the soured cream then gradually whisk in the cooled gelatine liquid. Spread the cream mixture over the top of the cold cake and level the surface. Chill in the refrigerator for 2 hours, or until the cream topping is set.

5. To decorate, carefully lift the cake out of the tin, using the lining paper to help you. Lay thin strips of paper in a random pattern over the topping. Mix together the icing sugar and cocoa powder and sift over the strips of paper. Lift the paper strips away and cut the cake into squares.

Tea for two
&
a slice of cake

Rhubarb Meringue Squares

1. Preheat the oven to 180°C/350°F/Gas Mark 4. Grease a 23-cm x 33-cm/9-inch x 13-inch Swiss roll tin and line with baking paper.

2. Sift the flour into a large bowl and add the diced butter. Rub the butter into the flour until it resembles coarse breadcrumbs. Stir in the sugar and egg and mix with a round-bladed knife until beginning to clump together.

3. Turn the crumbly dough into the prepared tin and, using lightly floured hands, press out firmly in an even layer in the base of the tin. Smooth level with the back of a spoon. Bake in the preheated oven for 15 minutes until pale golden.

4. To prepare the filling, place the chopped rhubarb in a bowl and stir in the sugar and raspberries. Spread over the baked base and return to the oven for 30 minutes. Remove from the oven and increase the oven temperature to 200°C/400°F/Gas Mark 6.

5. To make the meringue, place the egg whites in a bowl and whisk until holding stiff peaks. Gradually whisk in the sugar, one spoonful at a time, until you have a firm glossy meringue.

6. Spread the meringue over the top of the fruit and right to the edges of the tin. Return the tin to the oven and bake for a further 5–10 minutes, or until the top of the meringue is golden. Serve warm or cold cut into squares straight from the tin, dusted with icing sugar.

Makes 15

Ingredients
225 g/8oz plain flour,
   plus extra for dusting
150 g/5 ½ oz butter, at room
   temperature, diced,
   plus extra for greasing
85 g/3 oz caster sugar
1 large egg, lightly beaten

For the Filling
500 g/1lb 2 oz young pink
   rhubarb stalks, trimmed and
   cut into 2-cm/¾-inch pieces
4 tbsp caster sugar
115 g/4 oz frozen raspberries

For the Meringue
3 large egg whites
125 g/4 ½ oz caster sugar
icing sugar, for dusting

Caramel Squares

Makes 16

Ingredients

115 g/4 oz butter, softened,
  plus extra for greasing
55 g/2 oz caster sugar
175 g/6 oz plain flour
55 g/2 oz ground almonds

For the Topping

175 g/6 oz butter
115 g/4 oz caster sugar
3 tbsp golden syrup
400 ml/14 fl oz canned
  condensed milk
¼ tsp sea salt crystals
85 g/3 oz plain chocolate,
  melted

1. Preheat the oven to 180°C/350°F/Gas Mark 4. Grease a 20-cm/ 8-inch shallow square cake tin.

2. Put the butter and sugar into a bowl and beat together until pale and creamy. Sift in the flour and add the ground almonds. Use clean hands to mix and knead to a crumbly dough. Press into the base of the prepared tin and prick the surface all over with a fork. Bake in the preheated oven for 15 minutes, or until pale golden. Leave to cool.

3. To make the topping, put the butter, sugar, golden syrup and condensed milk into a saucepan over a low heat and heat gently until the sugar has dissolved. Increase the heat to medium, bring to the boil, then simmer for 6–8 minutes, stirring constantly, until the mixture becomes very thick. Stir in half the salt, then quickly pour the caramel over the shortbread base. Sprinkle over the remaining salt.

4. Spoon the chocolate into a paper piping bag and snip off the end. Pipe the chocolate over the caramel and swirl with the tip of a knife. Leave to cool, then chill for 2 hours, or until firm. Cut into 16 squares.

Coconut Jam Squares

1. Preheat the oven to 180°C/350°F/Gas Mark 4. Grease a 23-cm/9-inch shallow square cake tin.

2. Beat the butter and sugar together in a large bowl until fluffy. Beat in the egg yolk, then sift in the flour and mix to a soft dough. Knead lightly, then press into the base of the prepared tin. Prick all over with a fork and bake in the preheated oven for 20–25 minutes, or until pale golden.

3. To make the topping, put the egg whites into a large bowl and whisk until holding stiff peaks. Gradually whisk in the sugar to make a firm, glossy meringue. Fold in two thirds of the coconut. Spread the jam over the cooked base in the tin, then spoon the meringue over the jam. Sprinkle with the remaining coconut.

4. Return to the oven for 15–20 minutes, or until the top of the meringue is crisp and golden. Leave to cool in the tin, then dust with cocoa powder, if using, and cut into 9 squares.

Makes 9

Ingredients

150 g/5½ oz butter, softened, plus extra for greasing
70 g/2½ oz caster sugar
1 large egg yolk
200 g/7 oz plain flour
6 tbsp seedless raspberry jam
cocoa powder, to dust (optional)

For the Coconut Topping
2 large egg whites
115 g/4 oz caster sugar
40 g/1½ oz desiccated coconut

Raspberry Mousse Squares

Makes 12

Ingredients

115 g/4 oz butter, softened,
*   plus extra for greasing*
115 g/4 oz caster sugar
1 tsp vanilla extract
2 eggs, lightly beaten
115 g/4 oz self-raising flour
1 tbsp milk

For the Mousse

4 leaves of gelatine
450 g/1 lb fresh raspberries,
*   plus extra for decoration*
85 g/3 oz caster sugar
300 ml/10 fl oz double cream
2 tbsp flaked almonds, toasted
icing sugar, for dusting

1. Preheat the oven to 180°C/350°F/Gas Mark 4. Grease a 28-cm x 18-cm/11-inch x 7-inch traybake tin and line the base with baking paper.

2. Place the butter, sugar and vanilla extract in a large bowl and, using a hand-held electric whisk, beat together until pale and creamy. Gradually beat in the eggs.

3. Sift over the flour and fold into the mixture with the milk until thoroughly combined. Spread the mixture in an even layer in the prepared tin.

4. Bake in the preheated oven for 18–20 minutes, or until risen and golden and just firm to the touch. Leave to cool in the tin for 10 minutes then turn out onto a wire rack, peel off the lining paper and leave to cool completely.

5. To make the mousse, soak the gelatine leaves in a bowl of cold water for 10 minutes until soft. Press 150 g/5½ oz of the raspberries through a fine-holed sieve to make a smooth purée.

6. Place the purée in a small saucepan with the sugar. Remove the gelatine leaves from the water and squeeze out the excess liquid. Add to the purée and heat gently, stirring all the time, until the gelatine has dissolved. Leave to cool for 15 minutes.

7. Pour the cream into a large bowl and whip until holding firm peaks. Gradually whisk in the purée. Lightly crush the remaining raspberries with a fork and fold into the cream mixture.

8. Return the cold sponge to the traybake tin. Spread the raspberry mixture over the top of the sponge in an even layer. Chill in the refrigerator for 2–3 hours, or until set. Decorate with flaked almonds and raspberries, and dust lightly with icing sugar. Cut into squares to serve.

Raspberry Sponge Roll

1. Preheat the oven to 180°C/350°F/Gas Mark 4. Grease and line a 23-cm x 33-cm/9-inch x 13-inch Swiss roll tin with the paper 1 cm/½ inch above the rim. Lay a sheet of baking paper on the work surface and sprinkle with caster sugar.

2. Sift the flour and baking powder into a large bowl and add the butter, sugar, eggs and vanilla extract. Beat well until the mixture is smooth, then beat in the milk.

3. Spoon the mixture into the prepared tin and smooth into the corners with a palette knife. Bake in the preheated oven for 15–20 minutes, or until risen, firm and golden brown.

4. When cooked, turn the sponge out onto the sugared baking paper and spread with the jam. Roll up the sponge firmly from one short side to enclose the jam, keeping the paper around the outside to hold it in place.

5. Lift onto a wire rack to cool, removing the paper when firm. Sprinkle with caster sugar, cut into slices and serve.

Serves 8

Ingredients
*oil or melted butter,
  for greasing*
150 g/5½ oz plain white flour
1½ tsp baking powder
*175 g/6 oz unsalted butter,
  softened*
*175 g/6 oz caster sugar, plus
  extra for sprinkling*
3 eggs, beaten
1 tsp vanilla extract
2 tbsp milk
*115 g/4 oz raspberry jam,
  warmed*

Blueberry Slices

Serves 12

Ingredients
250 g/9 oz plain flour,
  plus extra for dusting
1 tsp baking powder
175 g/6 oz butter, at room
  temperature, diced,
  plus extra for greasing
85 g/3 oz caster sugar
1 egg, lightly beaten

For the Topping
2 eggs
150 ml/5 fl oz whipping cream
55 g/2 oz caster sugar
4 tbsp blueberry jam
200 g/7 oz fresh blueberries

1. Preheat the oven to 180°C/350°F/Gas Mark 4. Grease a 23-cm x 33-cm/9-inch x 13-inch Swiss roll tin and line with baking paper.

2. Sift the flour and baking powder into a large bowl and add the diced butter. Rub the butter into the flour until it resembles coarse breadcrumbs. Stir in the sugar and egg and mix with a round-bladed knife until beginning to clump together.

3. Gather the dough together and knead lightly on a floured surface. Press the dough out in an even layer in the base of the tin, using floured hands. Prick all over with the prongs of a fork.

4. Bake in the preheated oven for 15 minutes until pale golden. Remove from the oven and leave to cool. Leave the oven switched on.

5. To make the topping place the eggs, cream and sugar in a bowl and whisk together until smooth.

6. Spread the jam over the part-baked base then gently spoon over the eggs and cream mixture. Scatter over the blueberries and return to the oven for 25 minutes, or until the topping is set and pale golden. Serve warm or cold, sliced, from the tin.

Redcurrant Crumble Squares

1. Preheat the oven to 180°C/350°F/Gas Mark 4. Grease a 28-cm x 18-cm/11-inch x 7-inch traybake tin and line the base with baking paper.

2. Sift the flour into a large bowl and add the butter. Rub the butter into the flour until the mixture resembles coarse breadcrumbs. Stir in the sugar and make a well in the centre. Add the egg and milk and mix with a round-bladed knife to a soft, crumbly dough. Knead lightly on a floured surface.

3. Use floured hands to press the dough out evenly in the base of the prepared tin. Spread the redcurrants on top.

4. To make the crumble topping, place the flour and butter in a bowl and rub the butter into the flour until the mixture resembles coarse breadcrumbs. Stir in the sugar.

5. Scatter the crumble mixture over the redcurrants. Bake in the preheated oven for 40–45 minutes, or until a skewer inserted into the cake comes out clean.

6. Leave the cake to cool in the tin for 20 minutes then transfer to a wire rack. Serve warm or cold, dusted with icing sugar, cut into squares and decorated with redcurrant sprigs, if liked.

Makes 12

Ingredients
225 g/8 oz self-raising flour, plus extra for dusting
100 g/3½ oz butter, at room temperature, diced, plus extra for greasing
100 g/3½ oz caster sugar
1 egg, lightly beaten
1 tbsp milk
300 g/10½ oz fresh redcurrants, removed from stalks

For the Crumble
85 g/3 oz self-raising flour
50 g/1¾ oz butter, at room temperature, diced
50 g/1¾ oz caster sugar
icing sugar, for dusting
redcurrant sprigs, for decoration (optional)

Gooseberry Squares

Makes 15

Ingredients

butter, for greasing
200 g/7 oz strong plain white
  flour, plus extra for dusting
1 tsp easy-bake dried yeast
25 g/1 oz caster sugar
100 ml/3½ fl oz hand-hot milk
1 egg, lightly beaten

For the Filling

350 g/12 oz medium-fat soft
  cheese or Quark
2 tbsp cornflour
85 g/3 oz caster sugar
2 eggs, lightly beaten
finely grated zest of ½ lemon
225 g/8 oz small fresh
  gooseberries, topped
  and tailed

For the Crumble Topping

70 g/2½ oz plain flour
40 g/1½ oz butter, at room
  temperature, diced
55 g/2 oz caster sugar
finely grated zest of ½ lemon
icing sugar, for dusting

1. Grease a 23-cm x 33-cm/9-inch x 13-inch Swiss roll tin. Place the flour in a large bowl and stir in the dried yeast and sugar. Make a well in the centre.

2. Pour the milk and egg into the well and mix with a round-bladed knife to make a soft sticky dough. Turn the dough onto a lightly floured surface and knead for 7–8 minutes until smooth and elastic, adding a little more flour if the dough is sticky.

3. Place the dough in a clean bowl. Cover with greased cling film and leave in a warm place for about 1¼ hours until the dough has almost doubled in size.

4. Turn the dough out onto a lightly floured surface and re-knead for 1 minute. Roll out to a rectangle almost as large as the prepared tin. Place the dough in the tin and push it into the corners with your fingertips. Cover with greased clingfilm and leave in a warm place for 30 minutes until puffy. Preheat the oven to 180°C/350°F/ Gas Mark 4.

5. To make the filling, place the soft cheese in a large bowl and whisk in the cornflour, sugar, eggs and lemon zest until smooth.

6. Spread the filling over the top of the dough then scatter over the gooseberries, pressing them down gently.

7. To make the crumble, place the flour and butter in a bowl and using your fingertips rub the butter into the flour until it resembles coarse breadcrumbs. Stir in the caster sugar and lemon zest. Sprinkle over the filling.

8. Bake in the preheated oven for 55 minutes–1 hour 5 minutes, or until the crumble topping is light golden and the filling is set. Serve warm or cold, cut into squares and dusted with icing sugar.

Strawberry Cake

1. Preheat the oven to 200°C/400°F/Gas Mark 6. Grease a 23-cm x 33-cm/9-inch x 13-inch Swiss roll tin and line with baking paper.

2. Place the eggs and sugar in a large heatproof bowl set over a saucepan of simmering water. Using an electric hand-held mixer, whisk together until the mixture is very thick and pale and leaves a trail on the surface when the beaters are lifted. Remove the bowl from the saucepan and whisk for a further 2–3 minutes.

3. Sift over half the flour and fold in gently. Fold in the hot water, then sift over the remaining flour and fold in. Spoon the mixture into the prepared tin and gently level the surface with a palette knife. Bake in the preheated oven for 9–10 minutes, or until risen, golden and springy to the touch. Leave to cool in the tin for 10 minutes then turn out onto a wire rack, peel off the lining paper and leave to cool completely.

4. To make the filling, blend the eggs yolks, custard powder and 4 tablespoons of the milk in a bowl until smooth. Pour the rest of the milk into a saucepan and bring to the boil then pour the hot milk onto the egg mixture and whisk together. Pour the mixture back in to the saucepan, add the sugar and bring to the boil, whisking all the time, until smooth and thick. Transfer the custard to a bowl, cover the surface with clingfilm and leave to cool completely. Beat the cold custard until smooth then fold in the whipped cream and vanilla extract.

5. Return the cold sponge to the baking tin and spread the cream custard over the top. Arrange the strawberries, pointed side up, on top. Place the gelatine and water in a small saucepan and leave for 10 minutes until the gelatine is soft. Add the sugar and lemon juice and heat gently, stirring, until the gelatine has dissolved. Transfer to a bowl and leave to cool for 15–20 minutes or until just beginning to thicken. Brush the glaze all over the strawberries and sprinkle over the chopped pistachios. Leave in a cool place until the glaze has set, then cut into slices to serve.

Serves 15

Ingredients
butter, for greasing
3 eggs
125 g/4 ½ oz caster sugar
125 g/4 ½ oz plain flour
1 tbsp hot water

For the Filling
2 egg yolks
2½ tbsp custard powder
250 ml/9 fl oz milk
85 g/3 oz caster sugar
125 ml/4 fl oz whipping cream,
   softly whipped
1 tsp vanilla extract

For the Topping & Glaze
750 g/1lb 10 oz medium-sized
   strawberries, hulled
1 leaf of gelatine
5 tbsp water
2 tbsp caster sugar
1 tsp lemon juice
2 tbsp pistachio nuts,
   finely chopped

Peach Squares

Makes 12

Ingredients

250 g/9 oz self-raising flour,
    plus extra for dusting
200 g/7 oz butter, at room
    temperature, diced, plus extra
    for greasing
85 g/3 oz ground almonds
100 g/3½ oz caster sugar
1 large egg, lightly beaten

For the Topping

2 eggs
85 g/3 oz caster sugar
150 g/5½ oz crème fraiche
finely grated zest of 1 lemon
4 tbsp cornflour
410 g can peach halves in juice,
    drained
2 tbsp flaked almonds
icing sugar, for dusting

1. To make the base, sift the flour into a large bowl and add the butter. Using your fingertips rub the butter into the flour until the mixture resembles coarse breadcrumbs. Stir in the ground almonds and sugar. Make a well in the centre, add the egg and mix with a round-bladed knife to form a soft dough. Knead lightly until just smooth, adding a little extra flour if necessary. Wrap the dough in clingfilm and chill in the refrigerator for 30 minutes.

2. Preheat the oven to 180°C/350°F/Gas Mark 4. Grease a 23-cm x 33-cm/9-inch x 13-inch Swiss roll tin.

3. Place the dough in the prepared tin and, using clean, lightly floured hands, press the dough in a even layer into the base and up the sides of the tin. Bake in the preheated oven for 15 minutes.

4. While the base is baking, prepare the topping. Place the eggs and caster sugar in a bowl and whisk together until thoroughly combined. Whisk in the crème fraiche, lemon zest and cornflour.

5. Remove the part-baked base from the oven. Cut the peach halves into quarters and arrange on the base. Carefully spoon the topping mixture over the peaches then scatter over the flaked almonds.

6. Return the tin to the oven and bake for a further 25–35 minutes, or until the topping is set and light golden. Leave in the tin to cool. Serve warm or cold, cut into squares and dusted with icing sugar.

Orange Slices

1. Preheat the oven to 190°C/375°F/Gas Mark 5. Grease a 20-cm x 30-cm/8-inch x 12-inch baking tray and sprinkle with the extra sponge cake crumbs.

2. To make the base, use an electric mixer to whisk the egg yolks with half of the sugar and the orange rind until fluffy. Beat the egg whites until forming firm peaks, gradually whisking in the remaining sugar as you beat. Fold the whipped egg white into the egg yolk mixture. Add the cake crumbs with the flour, ground almonds and melted butter and mix to combine.

3. Spoon the mixture into the prepared baking tray and smooth it flat. Bake in the preheated oven for about 40–45 minutes. Leave to cool in the tray for 5 minutes and then transfer to a wire rack to cool completely.

4. To make the glaze, put the sugar, apricot jam, orange juice, orange liqueur (if using) and orange zest in a saucepan. Boil it down to about two thirds of the original volume and brush over the cake. Cut the cake into slices and serve.

Makes 12

Ingredients
2 eggs, separated
125 g/4½ oz sugar
grated rind of 1 orange
25 g/1 oz sponge cake crumbs,
 plus extra for sprinkling
15 g/½ oz plain flour
85 g/3 oz ground almonds
15 g/½ oz butter, melted,
 plus extra for greasing

For the glaze
6 tbsp caster sugar
2½ tbsp apricot jam
250 ml/9 fl oz orange juice
1 tbsp orange liqueur (optional)
pared zest of 1 large orange

Chocolate Flapjacks

Makes 12

Ingredients

175 g/6 oz butter,
  plus extra for greasing
115 g/4 oz soft light
  brown sugar
3 tbsp golden syrup
1 tbsp stem ginger syrup
2 pieces stem ginger,
  finely chopped
350 g/12 oz rolled oats

For the Chocolate Glaze

175 g/6 oz plain chocolate,
  broken into pieces
40 g/1½ oz butter

1. Preheat the oven to 180°C/350°F/Gas Mark 4. Grease a 20-cm x 30-cm/8-inch x 12-inch shallow baking tin.

2. Put the butter, sugar, golden syrup and stem ginger syrup into a large saucepan over a low heat and heat gently until melted. Remove from the heat and stir in the ginger and oats.

3. Spoon the mixture into the prepared tin and smooth the surface. Bake in the preheated oven for 15–20 minutes, or until pale golden. Leave to cool in the tin.

4. To make the glaze, put the chocolate and butter into a heatproof bowl set over a saucepan of simmering water and heat until melted. Stir until smooth, then spread over the cooled flapjacks. Chill in the refrigerator for 1 hour, or until set. Cut into 12 bars.

Chocolate Cheesecake Bars

1. Preheat the oven to 160°C/325°F/Gas Mark 3. Grease a 20-cm x 30-cm/8-inch x 12-inch baking tray which is at least 5-cm/2-inches deep.

2. To make the base, sift together the flour, baking powder and cocoa powder in a large bowl. Rub in the butter and sugar then add the egg. Mix to a crumbly dough.

3. Spread three quarters of the mixture on the prepared baking tray, pressing firmly into the base and up the sides. Put the remainder of the base mixture to one side.

4. To make the filling, beat the butter, sugar and vanilla extract together in a large bowl. Gradually beat in the eggs. Add the cheese, cream and cornflour and beat until smooth.

5. Spread the cheesecake mixture onto the base and smooth flat with a spatula. Break the reserved crumble mixture apart with your fingertips and sprinkle over the top.

6. Bake in the preheated oven for 1¼ hours. Leave to cool completely before removing carefully from the baking tray. Dust with icing sugar, sprinkle with chopped hazelnuts and cut into bars before serving.

Makes 12

Ingredients
250 g/9 oz plain flour
2 tsp baking powder
3 tbsp cocoa powder
140 g/5 oz butter, cut into small
  dice, plus extra for greasing
140 g/5 oz caster sugar
1 egg

For the filling
250 g/9 oz butter, softened
280 g/10 oz caster sugar
2 tsp vanilla extract
4 eggs, lightly beaten
750 g/1 lb 10 oz medium-fat
  soft cheese or Quark
100 ml/3½ fl oz whipping cream
1 tbsp cornflour
icing sugar and chopped
  hazelnuts, for sprinkling

Cheesecakes & Cakes

Blueberry Cheesecake

Serves 10

Ingredients

sunflower oil, for brushing
85 g/3 oz butter
200 g/7 oz digestive biscuits,
  finely crushed
400 g/14 oz cream cheese
2 large eggs
140 g/5 oz caster sugar
1½ tsp vanilla extract
450 ml/16 fl oz soured cream

For the Topping

55 g/2 oz caster sugar
4 tbsp water
250 g/9 oz fresh blueberries
1 tsp arrowroot

1. Preheat the oven to 190°C/375°F/Gas Mark 5. Brush a 20-cm/8-inch round springform cake tin with oil.

2. Melt the butter in a saucepan over a low heat. Stir in the biscuits, then press into the base of the prepared tin.

3. Place the cream cheese, eggs, 100 g/3½ oz of the sugar and ½ teaspoon of the vanilla extract in a food processor. Process until smooth. Pour over the biscuit base and smooth the top. Place on a baking sheet and bake in the preheated oven for 20 minutes, or until set. Remove from the oven and leave for 20 minutes. Leave the oven switched on.

4. Mix the soured cream with the remaining sugar and vanilla extract in a bowl. Spoon over the cheesecake. Return it to the oven for 10 minutes, leave to cool, then cover with clingfilm and chill in the refrigerator for 8 hours, or overnight.

5. To make the topping, place the sugar and 2 tablespoons of the water in a saucepan over a low heat and stir until the sugar has dissolved. Increase the heat, add the blueberries, cover and cook for a few minutes, or until they begin to soften. Remove from the heat. Mix the arrowroot and remaining water in a bowl, add to the blueberries and stir until smooth. Return to a low heat. Cook until the juice thickens and turns translucent. Leave to cool. Remove the cheesecake from the tin 1 hour before serving. Spoon over the blueberry topping and chill until ready to serve.

Classic Cheesecake

1. To make the base, sift the flour into a bowl and, using an electric mixer with a dough hook, beat in the sugar, vanilla extract and butter. Beat in the egg and knead to a smooth mixture. Form into a ball, wrap in clingfilm and place in the refrigerator for 1 hour.

2. Preheat the oven to 180°C/350°F/Gas Mark 4. Line the base of a 28-cm/11-inch springform cake tin with baking paper and grease the sides with a little butter.

3. Turn the dough out onto a floured surface and roll out to a thickness of about 5 mm/¼ inch. Line the base and the sides of the tin with the dough and prick the base with a fork several times. Bake in the preheated oven for about 15 minutes.

4. To make the topping, put the egg whites and sugar in a bowl and whisk until firmly peaking. In a separate bowl, beat together the cheese, cornflour, vanilla seeds, egg yolks, cream, lemon rind and juice. Fold the whisked egg white into the cheese mixture in two stages. This will help to make the cheesecake nice and light.

5. Spread the topping onto the partially baked base and smooth flat with a spatula. Return the cheesecake to the oven for about 1 hour. Take the cheesecake out of the oven and leave to cool in the tin. Then remove from the tin and dust with icing sugar to serve.

Serves 12

Ingredients
200 g/7 oz plain flour,
*   plus extra for dusting*
4½ tbsp caster sugar
1 tsp vanilla extract
115 g/4 oz butter, softened,
*   plus extra for greasing*
1 egg

For the Topping
5 eggs, separated
225 g/8 oz caster sugar
800 g/1 lb 12 oz medium-fat
*   soft cheese or Quark*
60 g/2¼ oz cornflour
seeds from 1 vanilla pod
300 ml/10 fl oz whipping cream
grated rind of 1 lemon
2 tbsp lemon juice
icing sugar, for dusting

Easy Cheesecake

Serves 8

Ingredients

20 g/¾ oz butter, for greasing
40 g/1½ oz fresh white
  breadcrumbs
750 g/1 lb 10 oz medium-fat
  soft cheese or Quark
100 ml/3½ fl oz soured cream
3 eggs
150 g/5½ oz caster sugar
4 tbsp cornflour
100 ml/3½ fl oz sunflower oil
100 ml/3½ fl oz milk
icing sugar, for dusting

1. Preheat the oven to 160°C/325°F/Gas Mark 3. Grease a 23-cm/9-inch diameter springform cake tin with butter and sprinkle the breadcrumbs over the base.

2. To make the cheesecake filling, mix the cheese, soured cream, eggs, sugar, cornflour, oil and milk together and beat to a smooth, creamy consistency.

3. Spoon the cheesecake mixture into the tin, smooth with a spatula, and bake in the preheated oven for 1 hour.

4. Leave the cheesecake to cool in the tin before removing and carefully placing on a serving plate. Dust with icing sugar to serve.

Caramel Pecan Cheesecake

1. Preheat the oven to 160°C/325°F/Gas Mark 3. Lightly grease a 23-cm/9-inch round springform cake tin.

2. Put the crushed biscuits and the nuts into a bowl and stir in the butter. Press into the base of the prepared cake tin. Chill in the refrigerator while making the filling.

3. Put the cheese and sugars into a large bowl and beat together until creamy. Gradually beat in the eggs and vanilla extract, then fold in the soured cream and cornflour. Pour over the biscuit base.

4. Place on a baking sheet and bake in the preheated oven for 45–50 minutes, or until just set (the middle should still wobble slightly). Turn off the heat, open the oven door and leave the cheesecake in the oven until cold. Chill in the refrigerator for 3–4 hours or overnight.

5. Unclip the tin and transfer the cheesecake to a serving plate. To make the topping, gently spread the dulce de leche over the top of the cheesecake and sprinkle with the nuts.

Serves 8

Ingredients
*225 g/8 oz digestive biscuits,
 finely crushed
25 g/1 oz pecan nuts,
 finely chopped
85 g/3 oz butter, melted,
 plus extra for greasing
550 g/1 lb 4 oz cream cheese
25 g/1 oz soft light brown sugar
100 g/3½ oz caster sugar
3 large eggs, beaten
1 tsp vanilla extract
300 ml/10 fl oz soured cream
2 tbsp cornflour*

For the Topping
*4 tbsp dulce du leche
25 g/1 oz pecan nuts, chopped*

Cherry Cheesecake

Serves 10

Ingredients

125 g/4½ oz butter, melted,
  plus extra for greasing
150 g/5½ oz medium-fat soft
  cheese or Quark
100 ml/3½ fl oz milk
100 g/3½ oz caster sugar
2 tsp vanilla extract
300 g/10½ oz plain flour,
  plus extra for dusting
2 tsp baking powder

For the Filling

250 g/9 oz cherries
60 g/2¼ oz butter, softened
100 g/3½ oz caster sugar
1 tsp vanilla extract
2 tbsp lemon juice
2 eggs, separated
500 g/1 lb 2 oz medium-fat soft
  cheese or Quark
100 g/3½ oz plain flour
1 tsp baking powder
3 tbsp cornflour

For the Topping

70 g/2½ oz flaked almonds
85 g/3 oz plain flour
40 g/1½ oz butter
50 g/2½ oz caster sugar
icing sugar, for dusting

1. Preheat the oven to 160°C/325°F/Gas Mark 3. Line the base of a 26-cm/10½-inch springform cake tin with baking paper and grease the sides with butter.

2. To make the base, first mix the melted butter with the cheese, milk, sugar and vanilla extract in a bowl. Sift together the flour and baking powder and beat into the cheese mixture. Knead the mixture vigorously on a floured surface and press the mixture into the base and up the sides of the tin. Place in the refrigerator.

3. To make the filling, remove the stalks from the cherries, then rinse and stone the cherries. Put the butter and half of the sugar in a large bowl and use an electric mixer, or balloon whisk, to beat until fluffy. Add the vanilla extract and lemon juice and continue beating. Beat the egg yolks into the butter mixture and beat in the cheese. Sift together the flour, baking powder and cornflour into another large bowl and then add the cheese mixture gradually, whisking continuously.

4. Remove the base from the refrigerator. Whisk the egg whites until stiff then whisk in the remaining sugar until firmly peaking. Use a spatula to fold the whipped egg white into the cheese mixture in two stages. Spread half of the filling over the base in the tin and place half of the cherries on top. Spread the remaining filling over the top and smooth flat. Place the remaining cherries on top.

5. To make the topping, mix the almonds, flour, butter and sugar in a bowl and rub with your fingers until crumbly. Sprinkle the crumble mixture on top of the cheesecake filling.

6. Bake in the preheated oven for about 40 minutes, covering with foil towards the end of the cooking time. Leave the cooked cheesecake to rest in the tin for about 30 minutes. Dust with icing sugar and serve.

Apple & Raisin Cheesecake

1. Start by preparing the raisins for the topping. Place the raisins in a small bowl, pour over the black tea and leave to soak for an hour.

2. To make the base, sift together the flour and baking powder into a bowl and stir in the sugar. Add the diced butter and rub into the flour mixture between your fingers until the mixture is loose and crumbly. Add the egg, vanilla extract and rum and knead vigorously to make a firm dough. Wrap in clingfilm and leave to rest in the refrigerator for 30 minutes.

3. Preheat the oven to 160°C/325°F/Gas Mark 3. Grease and line the base of a 28-cm/11-inch diameter springform cake tin and grease the sides.

4. Roll out the dough on a floured surface to the diameter of the tin, place the dough in the greased tin and prick with a fork several times. Bake in the preheated oven for about 20 minutes until lightly browned. Leave the oven switched on.

5. To make the filling, put the cheese, lemon juice and cornflour in a large bowl and beat together until smooth and creamy. In another bowl beat the eggs, sugar and vanilla extract until fluffy. Stir the egg mixture into the cheese mixture.

6. To make the topping, pour the soaked raisins into a sieve and leave to drain. Peel, quarter and core the apples. Use a knife to cut 4–5 crosses 5 mm/¼ inch deep in the outer side of each quarter.

7. Spoon the cheese mixture over the base in the tin and smooth flat with a spatula. Arrange the apple quarters on the cake and sprinkle the raisins on top. Return the cheesecake to the oven and bake for a further 50 minutes, then leave to cool and dust with icing sugar to serve.

Serves 12

Ingredients
250 g/9 oz plain flour,
   plus extra for dusting
large pinch of baking powder
70 g/2½ oz caster sugar
140 g/5 oz butter, cut into small
   dice, plus extra for greasing
1 egg, lightly beaten
1 tsp vanilla extract
4 tsp rum

For the Filling
750 g/1 lb 10 oz medium-fat
   soft cheese or Quark
2 tbsp lemon juice
4 tbsp cornflour
3 eggs
100 g/3½ oz caster sugar
1 tsp vanilla extract

For the Topping
4 tbsp raisins
100 ml/3½ fl oz tea (black)
4 medium-sized cooking apples
icing sugar, for dusting

Lemon Cheesecake

Serves 6

Ingredients

55 g/2 oz butter,
*   plus extra for greasing*
175 g/6 oz gingernut biscuits,
*   crushed*
3 lemons
300 g/10½ oz ricotta cheese
200 g/7 oz Greek-style yogurt
4 eggs, beaten
1 tbsp cornflour
100 g/3½ oz caster sugar
strips of lemon zest, to decorate
icing sugar, for dusting

1. Preheat the oven to 180°C/350°F/Gas Mark 4. Grease a 20-cm/ 8-inch round springform cake tin and line with baking paper.

2. Melt the butter in a saucepan and stir in the biscuit crumbs. Press into the base of the prepared cake tin. Chill until firm.

3. Meanwhile, finely grate the rind from the lemons into a bowl and squeeze the juice. Add the ricotta, yogurt, eggs, cornflour and caster sugar and whisk until a smooth batter is formed.

4. Carefully spoon the mixture into the tin. Bake in the preheated oven for 40–45 minutes, or until just firm and golden brown.

5. Cool the cheesecake completely in the tin, then run a knife around the edge to loosen and turn out onto a serving plate. Decorate with lemon zest and dust with icing sugar.

Mixed Berry Meringue Cake

1. Preheat the oven to 180°C/350°F/Gas Mark 4. Grease a 28-cm/11-inch diameter springform cake tin and lightly dust with flour. Put the egg whites in a bowl in the refrigerator to use later in the meringue.

2. To make the base, use an electric mixer to beat the egg yolks, sugar and vanilla extract in a bowl, until fluffy.

3. Bring the milk and butter to the boil in a small pan over medium heat, pour into the egg and sugar mixture and whisk together thoroughly until very thick. Sift together the flour and baking powder into the bowl and fold in gently.

4. Pour the cake mixture into the tin and bake in the preheated oven for about 18 minutes until pale golden. Remove from the oven and leave to cool for a short time. Leave the oven switched on.

5. To make the meringue, using a hand-held electric mixer whisk the egg whites until holding stiff peaks. Gradually whisk in the sugar, one tablespoon at a time until the mixture is firm and glossy. Fold in the cornflour. Pick through the berries, reserving 1 tablespoon of each kind, then gently fold the remaining berries into the meringue. Spread the fruity meringue mixture over the baked cake base.

6. Scatter the reserved berries on top of the meringue. Turn the oven up to 220°C/425°F/Gas Mark 7, place the cake on the middle shelf, and bake for a further 10–15 minutes. Dust with icing sugar when cool and then serve.

Serves 12

Ingredients
3 egg yolks
150 g/5½ oz caster sugar
2 tsp vanilla extract
100 ml/3½ fl oz milk
100 g/3½ oz butter, plus extra
  for greasing
280 g/10 oz plain flour,
  plus extra for dusting
2 tsp baking powder

For the Meringue
3 egg whites
100 g/3½ oz caster sugar
1 tsp cornflour
200 g/7 oz redcurrants,
  removed from stalks
200 g/7 oz blueberries
icing sugar, for dusting

Plum Cheesecake

Serves 10

Ingredients
250 g/9 oz plain flour, plus
   extra for dusting
½ tsp baking powder
125 g/4½ oz butter, cut into
   small dice, plus extra
   for greasing
1 egg
90 g/3¼ oz caster sugar
¼ tsp ground cinnamon

For the Filling
3 eggs
150 g/5½ oz sugar
1 tsp vanilla extract
juice of ½ lemon
750 g/1 lb 10 oz medium-fat
   soft cheese or Quark
3 tbsp cornflour

For the Topping
600 g/1 lb 5 oz plums
2 tbsp soft light brown sugar

1. To make the base, sift together the flour and baking powder in a bowl. Add the other ingredients and use your hands to knead the mixture to a smooth dough. Wrap the dough in clingfilm and leave to rest in the refrigerator for 30 minutes.

2. To make the filling, put the eggs, sugar and vanilla extract in a bowl and beat with an electric mixer or whisk until fluffy. Add the lemon juice, cheese and cornflour and mix until smooth and creamy.

3. Preheat the oven to 200°C/400°F/Gas Mark 6. Grease a 26-cm/10½-inch diameter springform cake tin and lightly dust with flour.

4. Remove the dough from the refrigerator, knead and roll on a lightly floured surface until it is 5 mm/¼ inch thick and slightly larger than the tin. Line the prepared tin with the dough, pressing up the sides, and prick the base with a fork several times. Spread the filling over the base and smooth using a palette knife. Bake in the preheated oven for approximately 30 minutes. Meanwhile, wash the plums, remove the stones and cut them into quarters.

5. Remove the cheesecake from the oven, leaving the oven switched on. Arrange the plums on top and sprinkle with the brown sugar. Return the cheesecake to the oven and bake for a further 40 minutes. Leave to cool then serve.

Mocha Cheesecake

1. Grease a 20-cm/8-inch round springform cake tin. Melt the butter in a large saucepan. Remove from the heat. Add the crushed biscuits and mix well. Spoon over the base of the prepared tin and press down evenly. Chill until firm.

2. Place the chocolate and the coffee liquid in a heatproof bowl. Set the bowl over a pan of gently simmering water until melted. Cool slightly. Pour the cold water into another heatproof bowl, sprinkle the gelatine evenly over the surface and leave for 5 minutes until spongy. Set the bowl over a pan of gently simmering water until melted. Remove from the heat.

3. Place the ricotta cheese, sugar and chocolate mixture in a large bowl, beat together with an electric hand-held whisk until smooth, then whisk in the melted gelatine. Fold in the cream, then spoon over the biscuit base. Chill for at least 3 hours or until firm.

4. Dredge the top of the cheesecake with sifted cocoa powder, remove from the tin and transfer to a serving plate. Serve with whipped cream.

Serves 6

Ingredients
85 g/3 oz butter, plus extra
  for greasing
200 g/7 oz chocolate
  digestive biscuits, crushed

For the Filling
175 g/6 oz plain chocolate,
  broken into pieces
1 tbsp instant espresso
  powder dissolved in
  90 ml/6 tbsp boiling water
90 ml/6 tbsp cold water
6 tsp powdered gelatine
375 g/13 oz ricotta cheese
85 g/3 oz caster sugar
225 ml/8 fl oz double cream,
  softly whipped
cocoa powder, to decorate
whipped cream, to serve

Apricot Cream Cake

Serves 12

Ingredients

250 g/9 oz plain flour
1 tsp baking powder
6 tbsp caster sugar
1 tsp vanilla extract
1 egg
125 g/4½ oz butter, plus extra
   for greasing

For the Filling

3 egg whites
200 ml/7 fl oz double cream
300 ml/10 fl oz soured cream
300 g/10½ oz medium-fat soft
   cheese or Quark
140 g/5 oz caster sugar
3 egg yolks
1 tbsp lemon juice
30 g/1 oz cornflour

For the Apricot Layer

500 g/1 lb 2 oz apricots
icing sugar, for dusting

1. To make the base, sift together the flour and baking powder in a bowl. Add the other ingredients and use your hands to knead the mixture to a smooth dough. Wrap the dough in clingfilm and leave to rest in the refrigerator for 30 minutes.

2. Preheat the oven to 180°C/350°F/Gas Mark 4. Grease a 28-cm/11-inch springform cake tin. Line the base of the prepared tin with half of the dough. Shape the remaining dough into a long roll and press around the edge of the dough base and against the side of the tin to create a 3 cm/1¼-inch raised rim. Bake the cheesecake base in the preheated oven for about 12 minutes, remove from the oven and leave to cool for 5 minutes. Lower the oven temperature to 160°C/325°F/Gas Mark 3.

3. To make the filling, put the egg whites in a bowl and use a hand-held electric mixer on its fastest setting to beat until it makes firm peaks. In another bowl, whip the double cream until firmly peaking. Put the soured cream, cheese, sugar, egg yolks, lemon juice and cornflour in a large bowl and beat together until smooth and creamy. Fold in the double cream and the egg whites carefully.

4. To make the apricot layer, rinse the apricots, cut in half and remove the stones. Arrange the fruit on the base. Cover with the cheese mixture and smooth using a palette knife.

5. Return the cheesecake to the oven and bake for a further 55 minutes at the lower temperature. Cover with foil after about 40 minutes to prevent the surface from getting too brown. Turn the oven off. Leave the baked cheesecake to stand in the oven with the door slightly open for about 15 minutes, then remove from the oven and leave to cool in the tin. Dust with icing sugar and serve.

Gooseberry Cream Cake

1. Sift the flour into a bowl and stir in the yeast and sugar. Add the butter and rub into the flour with your fingertips to make fine breadcrumbs. Make a well in the centre and pour in the hand-hot milk. Mix with a round-bladed knife to a soft dough.

2. Knead on a lightly floured surface for 5–6 minutes until smooth and elastic. Place the dough in a bowl, cover and leave in a warm place for about 1 hour, or until the dough has doubled in size.

3. Preheat the oven to 180°C/350°F/Gas Mark 4. Grease a 23-cm/9-inch round springform tin.

4. Turn the dough out onto a floured surface and knead for 1–2 minutes. Roll out to a 25-cm/10-inch circle and place in the prepared tin, gently easing the dough up the sides of the tin.

5. To make the filling, place the soft cheese, sugar and vanilla extract in a bowl and beat together until smooth. Gradually beat in the eggs then stir in the soured cream and orange zest.

6. Spoon the mixture into the tin, then scatter over the gooseberries. Place the tin on a baking sheet and bake in the preheated oven for 30 minutes.

7. To make the topping, place the egg and sugar in a bowl and, using a hand-held electric mixer, whisk together until pale and thick. Whisk in the melted butter, then sift over the flour and gently fold in.

8. Remove the cake from the oven and gently spoon the topping over the partially set filling. Return to the oven and bake for a further 25–30 minutes, or until the topping is set and golden. Leave to cool in the tin.

Serves 8

Ingredients
175 g/6 oz strong plain white flour, plus extra for dusting
1 tsp easy-bake dried yeast
25 g/1 oz caster sugar
25 g/1 oz butter, softened, plus extra for greasing
125 ml/4 fl oz hand-hot milk

For the Filling
200 g/7 oz medium-fat soft cheese
55 g/2 oz caster sugar
1 tsp vanilla extract
2 eggs, lightly beaten
300 ml/10 fl oz soured cream
grated zest of ½ orange
300 g/10½ oz fresh gooseberries, topped and tailed

For the Topping
1 egg, lightly beaten
40 g/1½ oz caster sugar
50 g/1¾ oz unsalted butter, melted
2 tbsp plain flour

Apple Caramel Upside Down Cake

Serves 6

Ingredients

oil or melted butter,
  for greasing
175 g/6 oz plain flour
1 tbsp baking powder
175 g/6 oz unsalted butter,
  softened
175 g/6 oz caster sugar
3 eggs, beaten
1 tsp vanilla extract
finely grated rind of 1 lemon

For the Toffee Apple Topping

55 g/2 oz unsalted butter
100 g/3½ oz caster sugar
1 tbsp water
4 eating apples
2 tbsp lemon juice

1. Preheat the oven to 180°C/350°F/Gas Mark 4. Grease a 23-cm/9-inch round cake tin with a solid base.

2. For the toffee apple topping, place the butter and sugar in a heavy-based saucepan with the water and heat gently until melted, then bring to the boil. Reduce the heat and cook, stirring, until it turns to a deep golden caramel colour. Pour quickly into the prepared tin, tilting to cover the base evenly.

3. Peel, core and thickly slice the apples, toss with the lemon juice and spread evenly over the base of the tin.

4. Sift the flour and baking powder into a large bowl and add the butter, sugar, eggs and vanilla extract. Beat well until the mixture is smooth, then stir in the lemon rind.

5. Spoon the mixture over the apples and smooth the surface with a palette knife. Bake in the preheated oven for 40–50 minutes, or until risen and golden brown.

6. Leave to cool in the tin for 2–3 minutes, then turn out carefully onto a warmed serving plate.

Iced Madeira Cake

1. Preheat the oven to 160°C/325°F/Gas Mark 3. Grease a 900-g/ 2-lb loaf tin and line with baking paper.

2. Place the butter and caster sugar in a large bowl and beat together until very pale and creamy. Beat in the lemon rind then gradually beat in the eggs. Sift the self-raising and plain flours into the mixture and fold in gently until thoroughly incorporated. Fold in the milk and lemon juice.

3. Spoon the mixture into the prepared tin and bake in the preheated oven for 1–1¼ hours, or until well risen, golden brown and a skewer inserted into the centre comes out clean. Cool in the tin for 15 minutes, then turn out onto a wire rack to cool completely.

4. For the icing, sift the icing sugar into a bowl. Add the lemon juice and stir to make a smooth and thick icing. Gently spread the icing over the top of the cake. Drizzle the warmed lemon curd over the icing and drag a skewer through the icing to create a swirled effect.

Serves 10

Ingredients
175 g/6 oz unsalted butter,
* softened, plus extra*
* for greasing*
175 g/6 oz caster sugar
finely grated rind of 1 lemon
3 eggs, lightly beaten
140 g/5 oz self-raising flour
115 g/4 oz plain flour
2 tbsp milk
1 tbsp lemon juice

For the Icing
175 g/6 oz icing sugar
2–3 tbsp lemon juice
2 tsp lemon curd, warmed

Red Velvet Cake

1. Preheat the oven to 190°C/375°F/Gas Mark 5. Grease two 23-cm/9-inch sandwich tins and line with baking paper.

2. Place the butter, water and cocoa powder in a small saucepan and heat gently, without boiling, stirring until melted and smooth. Remove from the heat and leave to cool slightly.

3. Beat together the eggs, buttermilk, vanilla extract and food colouring in a bowl until frothy. Beat in the butter mixture. Sift together the flour, cornflour and baking powder, then stir quickly and evenly into the mixture with the caster sugar.

4. Divide the mixture between the prepared tins and bake in the preheated oven for 25–30 minutes, or until risen and firm to the touch. Leave to cool in the tins for 3–4 minutes, then turn out onto a wire rack to cool completely.

5. To make the frosting, beat together all the ingredients until smooth. Use about half of the frosting to sandwich the cakes together, then spread the remainder over the top, swirling with a palette knife.

Serves 12

Ingredients
225 g/8 oz unsalted butter, plus extra for greasing
4 tbsp water
55 g/2 oz cocoa powder
3 eggs, beaten
250 ml/9 fl oz buttermilk
2 tsp vanilla extract
2 tbsp red edible food colouring
280 g/10 oz plain flour
55 g/2 oz cornflour
1½ tsp baking powder
280 g/10 oz caster sugar

For the Frosting
250 g/9 oz cream cheese
40 g/1½ oz unsalted butter
3 tbsp caster sugar
1 tsp vanilla extract

Marble Cake

Serves 8

Ingredients:
55 g/2 oz plain chocolate
3 tbsp milk
70 g/2½ oz unsalted butter,
  plus extra for greasing
85 g/3 oz caster sugar
1 egg, beaten
3 tbsp soured cream
115 g/4 oz self-raising flour,
  plus extra for dusting
½ tsp baking powder
½ tsp vanilla extract

1. Preheat the oven to 160°C/325°F/Gas Mark 3. Grease a 450-g/1-lb loaf tin and line the base with non-stick baking paper. Dust a little flour around the inside of the tin, shaking out the excess.

2. Break up the chocolate, place in a small heatproof bowl with the milk and set over a saucepan of simmering water. Heat gently until just melted. Remove from the heat.

3. Cream together the butter and sugar until light and fluffy. Beat in the egg and soured cream. Sift the flour and baking powder over the mixture, then fold in lightly and evenly using a metal spoon.

4. Spoon half the mixture into a separate bowl and stir in the chocolate mixture. Add the vanilla extract to the plain mixture. Spoon the chocolate and vanilla mixtures alternately into the prepared loaf tin, swirling lightly with a knife or skewer for a marbled effect. Bake in the preheated oven for 40–45 minutes, or until well-risen and firm to the touch.

5. Cool in the tin for 10 minutes, then turn out and finish cooling on a wire rack.

Classic Chocolate Cake

1. Preheat the oven to 180°C/350°F/Gas Mark 4. Grease two 20-cm/8-inch sandwich tins and line with baking paper.

2. Blend the cocoa powder and water to a smooth paste and set aside. Put the butter, caster sugar and brown sugar into a large bowl and beat together until pale and creamy. Gradually beat in the eggs, then stir in the cocoa paste and vanilla extract.

3. Sift in the flour and fold in gently. Divide the mixture between the prepared tins. Bake in the preheated oven for 25–30 minutes, or until risen and just springy to the touch. Leave to cool in the tins for 5 minutes, then turn out onto a wire rack to cool completely.

4. To make the frosting, put the chocolate and butter into a heat-proof bowl set over a saucepan of simmering water and heat until melted. Remove from the heat and stir in the cream. Leave to cool for 20 minutes, then chill in the refrigerator for 40–50 minutes, stirring occasionally, until thick enough to spread.

5. Sandwich the sponges together with one third of the frosting, then spread the remainder over the top and sides of the cake.

Serves 10

Ingredients
55 g/2 oz cocoa powder
7 tbsp boiling water
200 g/7 oz butter, softened,
  plus extra for greasing
125 g/4½ oz caster sugar
70 g/2½ oz soft light brown
  sugar
4 eggs, beaten
1 tsp vanilla extract
200 g/7 oz self-raising flour

For the Frosting
200 g/7 oz plain chocolate,
  broken into pieces
115 g/4 oz unsalted butter
100 ml/3½ fl oz double cream

Coffee Bundt Cake

Serves 14

Ingredients

400 g/14 oz plain flour,
  plus extra for dusting
1 tbsp baking powder
1 tsp bicarbonate of soda
3 tbsp espresso coffee powder
275 g/9¾ oz lightly salted
  butter, softened, plus extra
  for greasing
125 g/4½ oz light muscovado
  sugar
225 ml/8 fl oz maple syrup
3 eggs, beaten
225 ml/8 fl oz buttermilk
225 ml/8 fl oz double cream

For the Decoration

4 tbsp maple syrup
200 g/7 oz icing sugar
15 g/½ oz unsalted butter,
  melted
20 chocolate-coated coffee
  beans

1. Preheat the oven to 180°C/350°F/Gas Mark 4. Grease and lightly flour a 3-litre/5¼-pint Bundt tin.

2. Sift the flour, baking powder, bicarbonate of soda and coffee powder into a bowl. In a separate bowl, beat together the butter and muscovado sugar until pale and creamy. Gradually whisk in the maple syrup. Beat in the eggs slowly, adding 3 tablespoons of the flour mixture to prevent curdling.

3. Mix together the buttermilk and cream and add half to the butter mixture. Sprinkle in half of the flour mixture and fold gently together. Add the remaining buttermilk and flour mixtures and mix together gently until just combined.

4. Spoon the mixture into the prepared tin and smooth the surface. Bake in the preheated oven for about 50 minutes, or until well risen and a skewer inserted into the centre comes out clean. Leave in the tin for 10 minutes, then loosen with a knife and turn out onto a wire rack to cool completely.

5. To decorate, beat the maple syrup in a bowl with 150 g/5½ oz of the icing sugar and the butter, until smooth and thickly coating the back of a wooden spoon. Transfer the cake to a serving plate and spoon the icing around the top of the cake so it starts to run down the sides.

6. Beat the remaining icing sugar in a small bowl with 1½–2 teaspoons of water to make a smooth paste. Using a teaspoon, drizzle the icing over the cake. Scatter the coffee beans over the top.

Maple & Pecan Bundt Cake

1. Preheat the oven to 160°C/325°F/Gas Mark 3. Grease and lightly flour a 2-litre/3½-pint Bundt tin.

2. Put the butter and brown sugar into a bowl and beat together until pale and fluffy. Gradually beat in the eggs, then stir in the nuts, maple syrup and soured cream. Sift in the flour and fold in thoroughly.

3. Spoon the mixture into the prepared tin and gently smooth the surface. Bake in the preheated oven for 45–50 minutes, or until the cake is firm and golden and a skewer inserted into the centre comes out clean. Leave to cool in the tin for 10 minutes, then turn out onto a wire rack to cool completely.

4. To make the icing, mix the icing sugar, maple syrup and enough water to make a smooth icing. Spoon the icing over the top of the cake, allowing it to run down the sides. Decorate with the chopped nuts and leave to set.

Serves 10

Ingredients
200 g/7 oz butter, softened,
*   plus extra for greasing*
200 g/7 oz soft light brown
*   sugar*
3 large eggs, beaten
55 g/2 oz pecan nuts,
*   very finely chopped*
4 tbsp maple syrup
150 ml/5 fl oz soured cream
*   plus extra for dusting*
chopped pecan nuts,
*   to decorate*

For the Icing
85 g/3 oz icing sugar, sifted
1 tbsp maple syrup
1–2 tbsp lukewarm water

Lemon Drizzle Loaf

Serves 8–10

Ingredients
oil or melted butter,
  for greasing
175 g/6 oz plain flour
1 tbsp baking powder
175 g/6 oz unsalted butter,
  softened
175 g/6 oz golden caster sugar
3 eggs, beaten
1 egg yolk
finely grated rind of 1 lemon
2 tbsp lemon juice
fine strips of lemon zest,
  to decorate

For the Syrup
85 g/3 oz icing sugar
3 tbsp lemon juice

1. Preheat the oven to 180°C/350°F/Gas Mark 4. Grease and line a 1.2-litre/2-pint loaf tin.

2. Sift the flour and baking powder into a large bowl and add the butter, caster sugar, eggs and egg yolk. Beat well until the mixture is smooth, then stir in the lemon rind and juice.

3. Spoon the mixture into the prepared tin and smooth the surface with a palette knife. Bake in the preheated oven for 40–50 minutes, or until well risen, firm and golden brown.

4. Remove the tin from the oven and transfer to a wire rack. For the syrup, place the icing sugar and lemon juice in a saucepan and heat gently without boiling, stirring until the sugar dissolves.

5. Prick the top of the loaf several times with a skewer and spoon over the syrup. Leave to cool completely in the tin, then turn out, scatter with strips of lemon zest and cut into slices.

How to make the perfect cup of tea:

Fill your kettle with freshly drawn water and just before it reaches the boil, swirl some hot water in your teapot then discard. Use one heaped teaspoon of tea leaves per person plus one for the pot. Pour boiling water over the top and allow the tea to stand for 3-6 minutes, depending on the size of tea leaf. Give the pot a good stir before pouring through a strainer into cups. Add cold, fresh milk to taste.

Refrigerator Chocolate Cake

1. Grease and line a 450-g/1-lb loaf tin. Place the chocolate, butter, coffee, sugar and vanilla extract in a saucepan over a low heat and stir until the chocolate and butter have melted, the sugar has dissolved and the mixture is well combined.

2. Stir in the crushed biscuits, the raisins and walnuts and stir well.

3. Spoon the mixture into the prepared loaf tin. Leave to set for 1–2 hours in the refrigerator, then turn out and cut into thin slices to serve.

Serves 6–8

Ingredients
225 g/8 oz plain chocolate
225 g/8 oz unsalted butter,
  plus extra for greasing
3 tbsp black coffee
55 g/2 oz soft light brown sugar
a few drops of vanilla extract
225 g/8 oz digestive biscuits,
  crushed
85 g/3 oz raisins
85 g/3 oz walnuts, chopped

Carrot Cake

Serves 10

Ingredients

oil or melted butter,
* for greasing*
175 g/6 oz plain white flour
1 tbsp baking powder
1 tsp ground cinnamon
½ tsp ground ginger
175 g/6 oz unsalted butter,
* softened*
175 g/6 oz light muscovado
* sugar*
3 eggs, beaten
2 tbsp orange juice
200 g/7 oz carrots, coarsely
* grated*
55 g/2 oz pecan nuts, chopped,
* plus extra pecan halves*
* to decorate*

For the Frosting

55 g/2 oz full-fat soft cheese
250 g/9 oz icing sugar
finely grated rind of 1 orange
1 tbsp orange juice, plus extra
* if needed*

1. Preheat the oven to 160°C/325°F/Gas Mark 3. Grease and line a 23-cm/9-inch round deep cake tin.

2. Sift the flour, baking powder, cinnamon and ginger into a bowl and add the butter, muscovado sugar and eggs. Beat well until smooth, then stir in the orange juice, carrots and chopped pecan nuts.

3. Spoon the mixture into the prepared tin and smooth the top. Bake in the preheated oven for 1 hour–1 hour 10 minutes, or until risen, firm and golden brown.

4. Leave to cool in the tin for 10 minutes, then turn out onto a wire rack to to cool completely.

5. For the frosting, place all the ingredients in a bowl and beat until smooth and thick, adding more orange juice if necessary. Spread over the top of the cake and decorate with pecan halves.

Country Fruit Cake

1. Preheat the oven to 160°C/325°F/Gas Mark 3. Grease and line a 20-cm/8-inch round deep cake tin.

2. Sift the flours, baking powder and nutmeg into a large bowl, adding any bran left in the sieve. Add the butter, muscovado sugar, eggs and vanilla extract. Beat well until the mixture is smooth, then stir in the milk and mixed dried fruit.

3. Spoon the mixture into the prepared tin and smooth with a palette knife. Sprinkle the demerara sugar evenly over the surface. Bake in the preheated oven for 1 hour 20 minutes–1 hour 30 minutes, or until risen, firm and golden brown.

4. Leave to cool in the tin for about 20 minutes, then turn out onto a wire rack to cool completely.

Serves 10

Ingredients
oil or melted butter,
  for greasing
175 g/6 oz plain white flour
70 g/2½ oz plain wholemeal
  flour
2 tsp baking powder
½ tsp ground nutmeg
175 g/6 oz unsalted butter,
  softened
175 g/6 oz light muscovado
  sugar
3 eggs, beaten
1 tsp vanilla extract
1 tbsp milk
200 g/7 oz mixed dried fruit
1 tbsp demerara sugar

Boston Cream Pie

Serves 10

Ingredients
4 large eggs, beaten
115 g/4 oz caster sugar
115 g/4 oz plain flour
40 g/1½ oz butter, melted and
   cooled, plus extra for
   greasing

For the Pastry Cream
2 eggs
55 g/2 oz caster sugar
1 tsp vanilla extract
2 tbsp plain flour
2 tbsp cornflour
300 ml/10 fl oz milk
150 ml/5 fl oz double cream,
   softly whipped

For the Chocolate Glaze
115 g/4 oz plain chocolate,
   grated
1 tbsp golden syrup
25 g/1 oz unsalted butter
150 ml/5 fl oz double cream

1. Preheat the oven to 180°C/350°F/Gas Mark 4. Grease two 23-cm/9-inch sandwich tins and line with baking paper.

2. Place the eggs and sugar in a heatproof bowl set over a saucepan of simmering water. Using an electric hand-held whisk, beat together until the mixture is thick and pale and leaves a trail when the whisk is lifted.

3. Sift over the flour and fold in gently. Pour the butter in a thin stream over the mixture and fold in until just incorporated. Divide the mixture between the prepared tins and bake in the preheated oven for 20–25 minutes, or until light golden and springy to the touch. Cool in the tins for 5 minutes then turn out onto a wire rack to cool completely.

4. For the pastry cream, whisk together the eggs, sugar and vanilla extract. Blend the flour and cornflour to a paste with 4 tablespoons of the milk, then whisk into the egg mixture. Heat the remaining milk until almost boiling and pour onto the egg mixture, stirring all the time. Return to the saucepan and cook over a low heat, whisking all the time, until smooth and thickened. Pour into a bowl and cover with dampened greaseproof paper. Leave until cold, then fold in the whipped cream.

5. For the glaze, place the chocolate, golden syrup and butter in a heatproof bowl. Heat the cream until almost boiling, then pour over the chocolate. Leave for 1 minute, then stir until smooth.

6. To assemble, sandwich the sponges together with the pastry cream. Spread the chocolate glaze over the top of the cake.

Dessert
Cakes

Meringue Torte

Serves 12

Ingredients

300 g/10½ oz plain flour,
   plus extra for dusting
2 tsp baking powder
140 g/5 oz caster sugar
140 g/5 oz butter, room
   temperature, plus extra
   for greasing
2 eggs, lightly beaten

For the Topping

3 egg yolks
1 egg
100 g/3½ oz caster sugar
1 tbsp lemon juice
300 ml/10 fl oz milk
500 g/1 lb 2 oz medium-fat soft
   cheese or Quark
150 g/5½ oz butter, melted
5 tbsp custard powder

For the Meringue

3 egg whites
4 tbsp caster sugar
250 g/9 oz redcurrants,
   stems removed
icing sugar, for dusting

1. Preheat the oven to 160°C/325°F/Gas Mark 3. Grease a 28-cm/11-inch baking tin, preferably springform, and line the base with baking paper.

2. To make the base, sift together the flour and baking powder in a bowl, add the sugar, butter and eggs. Mix using an electric mixer with a dough hook attachment, then briefly knead with your hands into a smooth mixture. Wrap in clingfilm and leave to rest in the refrigerator for 30 minutes.

3. Use floured hands to press and smooth the mixture evenly into the base of the tin.

4. To make the topping, mix together the egg yolks, egg, sugar and lemon juice in a bowl. Gradually stir in the milk, cheese, melted butter and custard powder until the mixture is smooth and has no lumps.

5. Pour the topping mixture over the torte base and smooth the surface. Bake in the preheated oven for about 30 minutes. Remove the cake, but leave the oven switched on.

6. To make the meringue, whisk the egg whites until almost stiff. Gradually whisk in the sugar. Continue whisking until the sugar is completely dissolved and the meringue holds stiff peaks.

7. Spread the meringue over the topping. Scatter the redcurrants over the top. Return the torte to the oven to bake for about 15 minutes. Leave to cool before removing from the tin. Dust with icing sugar before slicing and serving.

Raspberry & Cream Gateau

1. Preheat the oven to 180°C/350°F/Gas Mark 4. Grease a 28-cm/ 11-inch springform cake tin.

2. To make the cake, using an electric mixer, whisk together the eggs and sugar in a bowl sitting over a pan of simmering water until very thick and the mixture leaves a trail when the beaters are lifted. Sift together the flour, cornflour and baking powder over the beaten egg mixture. Fold in gently.

3. Put the mixture into the base of the prepared tin and smooth using a palette knife. Bake in the preheated oven for 20 minutes, or until springy to the touch.

4. Leave the cake base to cool, then remove from the tin and cut in half horizontally using a long knife. Put the springform ring back round the lower cake base and set the other sponge half carefully aside.

5. To make the filling, soak the gelatine in a shallow bowl of cold water for 5 minutes until softened. Put the cheese, sugar, orange rind and orange juice in a bowl and whisk until smooth and creamy. Remove the gelatine from the water, squeezing out the excess liquid. Place the soft gelatine leaves in a small pan and heat very gently, stirring until completely dissolved. Remove from the heat and stir into the cheese mixture. Leave to cool.

6. Whip the double cream until it holds firm peaks. When the cheese mixture is almost set, carefully fold in the cream using a spatula. Spoon the raspberries over the cake base in the tin. Then spoon the cheese mixture into the tin and spread over the raspberries. Place the second sponge half on top with the cut side uppermost and gently press down. Chill the cake in the refrigerator for 3–4 hours.

7. To make the topping, whip the cream with the icing sugar until softly peaking. Remove the springform ring. Spread the cream over the gateau. Arrange the raspberries on top. Decorate with the grated chocolate and mint leaves and serve.

Serves 12

Ingredients
butter, for greasing
2 eggs
85 g/3 oz caster sugar
70 g/2½ oz plain flour
70 g/2½ oz cornflour
1 tsp baking powder

For the Filling
6 leaves of gelatine
750 g/1 lb 10 oz medium-fat
  soft cheese or Quark
150 g/5½ oz caster sugar
grated rind and juice of
  1 orange
500 ml/18 fl oz double cream
300 g/10½ oz fresh raspberries

For the Topping
200 ml/7 fl oz double cream
2 tbsp icing sugar
50 g/1¾ oz fresh raspberries
coarsely grated chocolate
  and fresh mint leaves,
  for decorating

Strawberry Gateau

Serves 8

Ingredients
2 large eggs
55 g/2 oz caster sugar
55 g/2 oz plain flour
25 g/1 oz butter, melted
* and cooled, plus extra*
* for greasing*

For the Filling
4 leaves of gelatine
finely grated zest and juice
* from 1 lemon*
200 g/7 oz medium fat soft
* cheese, or Quark*
125 g/4½ oz caster sugar
300 ml/10 fl oz double cream,
* softly whipped*

For the Topping
5 tbsp water
1 leaf of gelatine
2 tbsp caster sugar
1 tsp lemon juice
200 g/7 oz strawberries,
* hulled and sliced*
3–4 tbsp flaked almonds,
* toasted*

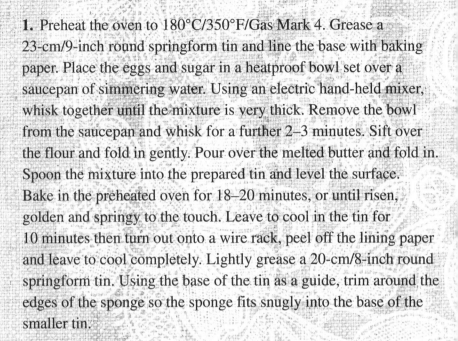

1. Preheat the oven to 180°C/350°F/Gas Mark 4. Grease a 23-cm/9-inch round springform tin and line the base with baking paper. Place the eggs and sugar in a heatproof bowl set over a saucepan of simmering water. Using an electric hand-held mixer, whisk together until the mixture is very thick. Remove the bowl from the saucepan and whisk for a further 2–3 minutes. Sift over the flour and fold in gently. Pour over the melted butter and fold in. Spoon the mixture into the prepared tin and level the surface. Bake in the preheated oven for 18–20 minutes, or until risen, golden and springy to the touch. Leave to cool in the tin for 10 minutes then turn out onto a wire rack, peel off the lining paper and leave to cool completely. Lightly grease a 20-cm/8-inch round springform tin. Using the base of the tin as a guide, trim around the edges of the sponge so the sponge fits snugly into the base of the smaller tin.

2. To make the filling, place the gelatine leaves in a bowl and cover with cold water. Leave to soak for 5 minutes until soft. Remove the leaves from the water and squeeze out the excess liquid. Place the leaves in a small pan with the lemon juice. Heat gently until the gelatine has completely dissolved. Leave to cool for 10 minutes. Place the soft cheese, sugar and lemon zest in a bowl and beat together smooth. Gradually beat in the gelatine mixture then fold in the whipped cream. Spoon over the sponge base, levelling the surface with a palette knife. Chill in the refrigerator for 1 hour. To make the topping, place the water and gelatine in a saucepan and leave for 10 minutes until the gelatine is soft. Add the sugar and lemon juice and heat gently, stirring, until the gelatine has dissolved. Transfer to a bowl and leave to cool for 15–20 minutes, or until just beginning to thicken. Arrange the sliced strawberries on top of the cream filling then spoon over the gelatine glaze. Chill in the refrigerator for a further 30 minutes until the glaze has set. Run a palette knife around the edge of the gateau, then unclip the tin and transfer the gateau to a serving plate. Gently press the flaked almonds around the sides.

Morello Cherry Gateau

1. Preheat the oven to 160°C/325°F/Gas Mark 3. Grease a 28-cm/11-inch round cake tin, preferably springform.

2. To make the cake, sift together the flour, sugar and cinnamon in a bowl. Add the diced butter and rub into the flour mixture between your fingers until the mixture resembles coarse breadcrumbs. Add the beaten egg and knead the mixture to a smooth dough. Wrap the mixture in clingfilm and leave to rest in the refrigerator for 30 minutes.

3. Roll the dough out on a floured surface, put it in the base of the prepared tin, press up the sides and prick several times with a fork. Bake in the preheated oven for about 20 minutes, or until lightly browned, and leave in the tin to cool. Leave the oven switched on.

4. To make the filling, mix together the cheese, lemon juice and cornflour in a bowl until smooth and creamy. Beat the eggs, sugar and vanilla extract until light and fluffy and stir into the cheese mixture.

5. Spoon the filling into the cake base. Arrange the drained cherries over the filling, and continue baking for a further 50 minutes until set and golden. Leave to cool. Dust with icing sugar before serving.

Serves 12

Ingredients
*250 g/9 oz self-raising flour,
 plus extra for dusting
90 g/3¼ oz caster sugar
large pinch of cinnamon
125 g/4½ oz cold butter,
 cut into small dice, plus extra
 for greasing
1 egg, lightly beaten*

For the filling
*750 g/1 lb 10 oz medium-fat
 soft cheese or Quark
2 tbsp lemon juice
55 g/2 oz cornflour
3 eggs, lightly beaten
125 g/4½ oz caster sugar
2 tsp vanilla extract*

For the topping
*350 g/12 oz (drained weight)
 Morello cherries from a jar
icing sugar, for dusting*

Double Chocolate Gateau

Serves 10

Ingredients

225 g/8 oz butter, softened,
  plus extra for greasing
225 g/8 oz golden caster sugar
4 eggs, beaten
225 g/8 oz self-raising flour
55 g/2 oz cocoa powder
a little milk (optional)

For the Filling

250 ml/9 fl oz whipping cream
225 g/8 oz white chocolate,
  broken into pieces

For the Icing

350 g/12 oz plain chocolate,
  broken into pieces
115 g/4 oz butter
100 ml/3½ fl oz double cream

For the Decoration

115 g/4 oz plain chocolate
  caraque
2 tsp icing sugar and cocoa
  powder, mixed

1. To make the filling, put the whipping cream in a saucepan and heat to almost boiling. Put the white chocolate in a food processor and chop. With the motor running, pour the hot cream through the feed tube and process for 10–15 seconds, until smooth. Transfer to a bowl, leave to cool, then cover with clingfilm and chill in the refrigerator for 2 hours, or until firm. Whisk until just starting to hold soft peaks.

2. Preheat the oven to 180°C/350°F/Gas Mark 4. Grease and line the base of a 20-cm/8-inch round deep cake tin. Put the butter and caster sugar in a bowl and beat until light and fluffy. Gradually beat in the eggs. Sift the flour and cocoa into a bowl, then fold into the mixture, adding milk, if necessary, to make a dropping consistency.

3. Spoon into the prepared tin and bake in the preheated oven for 45–50 minutes, until a skewer inserted into the centre comes out clean. Leave to stand in the tin for 5 minutes. Transfer to a wire rack to cool completely.

4. To make the icing, put the plain chocolate in a heatproof bowl set over a saucepan of gently simmering water until melted. Stir in the butter and double cream. Leave to cool, stirring occasionally until the mixture is a thick spreading consistency. Slice the cake horizontally into 3 layers. Sandwich the layers together with the white chocolate filling. Cover the top and sides of the cake with the icing and arrange the chocolate caraque over the top. Sift the mixed icing sugar and cocoa over the cake.

Orange Cheesecake Gateau

1. Preheat the oven to 180°C/350°F/Gas Mark 4. Grease and line two 23-cm/9-inch sandwich cake tins.

2. Sift the flour and baking powder into a large bowl and add the butter, caster sugar, eggs and orange flower water. Beat well until the mixture is smooth, then stir in the orange juice.

3. Spoon the mixture into the prepared tins and smooth the surfaces with a palette knife. Bake in the preheated oven for 25–30 minutes, or until risen and golden brown. Leave to cool in the tins for 5 minutes, then turn out onto a wire rack to cool completely.

4. Beat together all the filling ingredients until smooth, then spread about a third over one cake. Spoon the remainder into a piping bag fitted with a large star nozzle and pipe swirls around the edge of the cake.

5. Place the second cake on top. Pipe the remaining frosting around the top edge. Fill the centre with orange slices and brush with maple syrup.

Serves 8–10

Ingredients
oil or melted butter,
  for greasing
175 g/6 oz plain white flour
1 tbsp baking powder
175 g/6 oz unsalted butter,
  softened
175 g/6 oz golden caster sugar
3 eggs, beaten
1 tsp orange flower water
2 tbsp orange juice

For the Filling
600 g/1 lb 5 oz mascarpone
  cheese
finely grated rind of 1 orange
4 tbsp orange juice
55 g/2 oz icing sugar
1 tsp orange flower water

For the Topping
1 orange, peeled and sliced
maple syrup, for brushing

Walnut Gateau

Serves 8–10

Ingredients

oil or melted butter,
 for greasing
175 g/6 oz plain flour
1 tbsp baking powder
175 g/6 oz unsalted butter,
 softened
175 g/6 oz golden caster sugar
3 eggs, beaten
1 tsp vanilla extract
2 tbsp milk
125 g/4½ oz walnuts,
 finely chopped, plus extra
 walnut halves to decorate
3 tbsp apricot jam, warmed

For the Frosting

175 g/6 oz unsalted butter
350 g/12 oz icing sugar, sifted
100 ml/3½ fl oz single cream

1. Preheat the oven to 180°C/350°F/Gas Mark 4. Grease and base-line two x 20-cm/8-inch sandwich cake tins.

2. Sift the flour and baking powder into a large bowl and add the butter, caster sugar, eggs and vanilla extract. Beat well until the mixture is smooth, then stir in the milk and 40 g/1½ oz of the chopped walnuts.

3. Divide the mixture between the prepared tins and smooth the surfaces with a palette knife. Bake in the preheated oven for 25–30 minutes, or until risen, firm and golden brown.

4. Leave to cool in the tins for 2–3 minutes, then turn out onto a wire rack to cool completely. Slice each cake in half horizontally, to make four layers in total.

5. For the frosting, beat together the butter, icing sugar and cream until smooth. Spread about half the frosting over the top of three of the cakes and sandwich them together, placing the plain cake on top. Spread half the remaining frosting over the sides of the cake and press the remaining chopped walnuts over it.

6. Brush the apricot jam over the top of the cake. Spoon the remaining frosting into a piping bag fitted with a star nozzle and pipe swirls around the top. Decorate with walnut halves.

Almond & Hazelnut Gateau

1. Preheat the oven to 190°C/375°F/Gas Mark 5. Grease two 18-cm/7-inch sandwich tins and line with baking paper.

2. Whisk the eggs and caster sugar in a large mixing bowl with an electric hand-held whisk for about 10 minutes, or until the mixture is very light and foamy and a trail is left when the whisk is dragged across the surface. Fold in the ground nuts. Sift the flour and fold in with a metal spoon or palette knife. Divide the mixture between the prepared tins.

3. Scatter the flaked almonds over the top of one of the cakes. Bake both of the cakes in the preheated oven for 15–20 minutes, or until springy to the touch. Leave to cool slightly in the tins. Remove the cakes from the tins and transfer to a wire rack to cool completely.

4. Meanwhile, make the filling. Melt the chocolate in a heatproof bowl set over a saucepan of gently simmering water, remove from the heat and stir in the butter. Leave the mixture to cool slightly. Whip the cream until just holding its shape, then fold in the melted chocolate mixture.

5. Place the cake without the flaked almonds on a serving plate and spread the filling over it. Leave the filling to set slightly, then place the almond-topped cake on top and chill for about 1 hour. Dust with icing sugar and serve.

Serves 8

Ingredients
butter, for greasing
4 eggs
115 g/4 oz caster sugar
50 g/1¾ oz ground almonds
50 g/1¾ oz ground hazelnuts
50 g/1¾ oz plain flour
70 g/2½ oz flaked almonds
icing sugar, for dusting

For the Filling
100 g/3½ oz plain chocolate,
  broken into pieces
1 tbsp butter
300 ml/10 fl oz double cream

Chocolate & Cherry Gateau

Serves 8

Ingredients

oil or melted butter,
  for greasing
150 g/5½ oz plain white flour
2 tbsp cocoa powder
1 tbsp baking powder
175 g/6 oz unsalted butter,
  softened
175 g/6 oz golden caster sugar
3 eggs, beaten
1 tsp vanilla extract
2 tbsp milk
3 tbsp kirsch or brandy
  (optional)
grated chocolate and fresh
  whole cherries, to decorate

For the Filling and Topping

450 ml/16 fl oz double or
  whipping cream
2 tbsp icing sugar
225 g/8 oz fresh dark red
  cherries, stoned

1. Preheat the oven to 180°C/350°F/Gas Mark 4. Grease two 20-cm/8-inch sandwich cake tins and line the bases with baking paper.

2. Sift the flour, cocoa and baking powder into a large bowl and add the butter, caster sugar, eggs and vanilla extract. Beat well until the mixture is smooth, then stir in the milk.

3. Divide the mixture between the prepared tins and smooth the tops with a palette knife. Bake in the preheated oven for 25–30 minutes, or until risen and firm to the touch. Leave to cool in the tins for 2–3 minutes, then turn out onto a wire rack to cool completely.

4. When the cakes are cold, sprinkle with the kirsch, if using. Whip the cream with the icing sugar until thick, then spread about a third over the top of one of the cakes. Spread the cherries over the cream and place the second cake on top.

5. Spread the remaining cream over the top and sides of the cake and decorate with grated chocolate and fresh whole cherries.

Mississippi Mud Pie

1. Preheat the oven to 180°C/350°F/Gas Mark 4. Grease a 23-cm/9-inch springform or loose-based round cake tin.

2. To make the crumb crust, put the digestive biscuits, pecan nuts, sugar and cinnamon into a food processor and process until fine crumbs form – do not overprocess to a powder. Add the melted butter and process again until moistened.

3. Tip the crumb mixture into the prepared cake tin and press over the base and about 4 cm/1½ inches up the sides of the tin. Cover the tin and chill while you make the filling.

4. To make the filling, put the butter, chocolate and golden syrup into a saucepan over a low heat and stir until melted and blended. Leave to cool, then beat in the eggs and pecan nuts.

5. Pour the filling into the chilled crumb crust and smooth the surface. Bake in the preheated oven for 30 minutes, or until just set but still soft in the centre. Leave to cool on a wire rack. Serve at room temperature or chilled.

Serves 8

Ingredients
Crumb Crust
140 g/5 oz digestive biscuits
85 g/3 oz pecan nuts
1 tbsp soft light brown sugar
½ tsp ground cinnamon
85 g/3 oz butter, melted

For the Filling
225 g/8 oz butter or margarine,
  plus extra for greasing
175 g/6 oz plain chocolate,
  chopped
125 ml/4 fl oz golden syrup
4 large eggs, beaten
85 g/3 oz pecan nuts,
  finely chopped

Meringues!

Meringues are very versatile in baking, as they can be used to decorate cakes and desserts, as well as being lovely when eaten on their own or with a simple cream and jam filling.

To make 12 small meringues, place four eggs whites and a pinch of salt into the bowl of an electric mixer. Preheat the oven to 120°C/250°F/ Gas Mark ½ and line two baking trays with baking paper. Whisk the egg whites until soft peaks form, then gradually add in 200 g/7 oz caster sugar. Continue whisking until the mixture is very stiff. Place the mixture into a piping bag fitted with a plain nozzle and pipe 12 mounds onto the prepared baking trays. Bake in the preheated oven for about 1½ hours, then switch off the oven, leaving the meringues inside for half an hour before serving.

Sachertorte

Serves 10

Ingredients

175 g/6 oz plain chocolate,
  broken into pieces
140 g/5 oz unsalted butter,
  plus extra for greasing
140 g/5 oz caster sugar
6 eggs, separated
175 g/6 oz plain flour

For the Icing

225 g/8 oz plain chocolate,
  broken into pieces
5 tbsp strong black coffee
175 g/6 oz icing sugar
6 tbsp apricot jam, warmed

1. Preheat the oven to 150°C/300°F/Gas Mark 2. Grease and line a 23-cm/9-inch round springform cake tin.

2. Put the chocolate in a heatproof bowl set over a saucepan of gently simmering water until melted. In a separate bowl, beat the butter and 70 g/2½ oz of the sugar until pale and fluffy.

3. Add the egg yolks and beat well. Add the chocolate in a thin stream, beating well. Sift in the flour and fold it into the mixture. Whisk the egg whites until they stand in soft peaks. Add the remaining sugar and whisk until glossy. Fold half the egg white mixture into the chocolate mixture, then fold in the remainder.

4. Spoon into the prepared tin and smooth the top. Bake in the preheated oven for 1–1¼ hours, until a skewer inserted into the centre comes out clean. Cool in the tin for 5 minutes, then transfer to a wire rack to cool completely.

5. To make the icing, melt 175 g/6 oz of the chocolate and beat in the coffee until smooth. Sift in the icing sugar and whisk to give a thick icing. Halve the cake. Spread the jam over the cut edges and sandwich together. Invert the cake on a wire rack. Spoon the icing over the cake and spread to coat the top and sides. Leave to set for 5 minutes, letting any excess drop through the rack. Transfer to a serving plate and leave to set for at least 2 hours.

6. To decorate, melt the remaining chocolate and spoon into a small piping bag fitted with a fine plain nozzle. Pipe the word 'Sacher' or 'Sachertorte' on top of the cake. Leave to set before serving.

Black Forest Gateau

1. Preheat the oven to 200°C/400°F/Gas Mark 6. Line a 28-cm/ 11-inch round springform cake tin with baking paper.

2. To make the cake, put the egg whites, water and salt in a bowl and, using an electric mixer whisk until light and fluffy. Gradually whisk in the caster sugar and continue beating. Mix in the egg yolks and vanilla extract. Sift together the flour and cocoa powder into another bowl, then add to the egg mixture and fold in gently.

3. Pour the mixture into the baking tin and bake in the preheated oven for about 20–25 minutes until risen and just firm to the touch. Turn out onto a wire rack to cool, and remove the baking paper.

4. Cut the sponge horizontally into three equal layers. Drizzle 2 tablespoons of the kirsch over each layer.

5. To make the filling, drain the Morello cherries in a sieve, reserving the juice. Bring the cherry juice to the boil in a small saucepan with ½ tablespoon of the caster sugar. Combine the cornflour with a little water, stir into the cherry juice until dissolved and thickened. Add the cherries, remove from the hob, and leave to cool. Whip the cream with the vanilla extract and the remaining caster sugar until firmly peaking.

6. Spread a third of the whipped cream on the bottom cake layer, then arrange half of the cherries on top. Position the second layer on top, and spread with cream and cherries as above. Finally place the third layer on top. Spread whipped cream over the whole. Use a palette knife to coat the sides of the gateau with grated chocolate and scatter the rest over the top. Rest in the refrigerator for at least one hour before serving.

Serves 12

Ingredients
6 eggs, separated
6 tbsp warm water
pinch of salt
200 g/7 oz caster sugar
2 tsp vanilla extract
300 g/10½ oz self-raising flour
1 tbsp cocoa powder
6 tbsp kirsch
55 g/2 oz grated dark
  chocolate, for decorating

For the filling
350 g/12 oz Morello cherries
  from a jar
1½ tbsp caster sugar
1 tbsp cornflour
600 ml/1 pint whipping cream
2 tsp vanilla extract

Raspberry & Chocolate Cake

Serves 10

Ingredients

225 g/8 oz butter, plus extra
   for greasing
250 g/9 oz plain chocolate
1 tbsp strong black coffee
5 eggs
90 g/3¼ oz golden caster sugar
90 g/3¼ oz plain flour, sifted
1 tsp ground cinnamon
150 g/5½ oz fresh raspberries,
   plus extra to serve
cocoa powder, for dusting
whipped cream, to serve

1. Preheat the oven to 160°C/325°F/Gas Mark 3. Grease a 23-cm/9-inch round cake tin and line with baking paper.

2. Put the butter, chocolate and coffee in a heatproof bowl set over a saucepan of gently simmering water and heat until melted. Stir and leave to cool slightly.

3. Put the eggs and sugar in a bowl and beat until thick and pale. Gently fold in the chocolate mixture. Sift the flour and cinnamon into a bowl, then fold into the chocolate mixture. Pour into the prepared tin and sprinkle the raspberries evenly over the top.

4. Bake in the preheated oven for 35–45 minutes, until the cake is well risen and springy to the touch. Leave to cool in the tin for 15 minutes before turning out onto a large plate. Dust with cocoa and serve with raspberries and whipped cream.

Citrus Mousse Cake

1. Preheat the oven to 180°C/350°F/Gas Mark 4. Grease and line the base of a 20-cm/8-inch round springform cake tin.

2. Beat the butter and sugar in a bowl until light and fluffy. Gradually add the eggs, beating well after each addition. Sift together the flour and cocoa and fold into the creamed mixture. Fold in the melted chocolate.

3. Pour into the prepared tin and level the top. Bake in the preheated oven for 40 minutes, or until springy to the touch. Leave to cool for 5 minutes in the tin, then turn out onto a wire rack and leave to cool completely. Cut the cold cake horizontally into 2 layers.

4. To make the orange mousse, beat the egg yolks and sugar until pale, then whisk in the orange juice. Sprinkle the gelatine over the water in a small heatproof bowl and allow to go spongy, then place over a saucepan of hot water and stir until dissolved. Stir into the egg yolk mixture. Whip the cream until holding its shape, reserve a little for decoration, then fold the remainder into the orange mixture. Whisk the egg whites until standing in soft peaks, then fold in. Leave in a cool place until starting to set, stirring occasionally.

5. Place half of the cake back in the tin. Pour in the mousse and press the second cake layer on top. Chill until set. Transfer to a serving plate, spoon teaspoonfuls of cream around the top and decorate the centre with orange segments.

Serves 8

Ingredients
175 g/6 oz butter, plus extra
   for greasing
175 g/6 oz caster sugar
4 eggs, lightly beaten
200 g/7 oz self-raising flour
1 tbsp cocoa powder
50 g/1¾ oz orange-flavoured
   plain chocolate, melted
peeled orange segments,
   to decorate

For the Orange Mousse
2 eggs, separated
50 g/1¾ oz caster sugar
200 ml/7 fl oz freshly squeezed
   orange juice
2 tsp gelatine
3 tbsp water
300 ml/10 fl oz double cream

Small Bakes
& Breads

Classic Vanilla Cupcakes

Makes 12

Ingredients
175 g/6 oz unsalted butter,
  softened
175 g/6 oz caster sugar
3 large eggs, beaten
1 tsp vanilla extract
175 g/6 oz self-raising flour
hundreds and thousands,
  to decorate

For the Frosting
150 g/5 oz unsalted butter,
  softened
3 tbsp double cream or milk
1 tsp vanilla extract
300 g/10½ oz icing sugar,
  sifted

1. Preheat the oven to 180°C/350°F/Gas Mark 4. Place 12 paper cases in a muffin tin.

2. Put the butter and caster sugar into a bowl and beat together until pale and creamy. Gradually beat in the eggs and vanilla extract. Sift in the flour and fold in gently.

3. Divide the mixture evenly between the paper cases and bake in the preheated oven for 15–20 minutes, or until risen and firm to the touch. Transfer to a wire rack and leave to cool.

4. To make the frosting, put the butter into a bowl and beat with an electric mixer for 2–3 minutes, or until pale and creamy. Beat in the cream and vanilla extract. Gradually beat in the icing sugar and continue beating until the buttercream is light and fluffy.

5. Use a palette knife to swirl the frosting over the tops of the cupcakes. Decorate with hundreds and thousands.

Chocolate & Nut Cakes

1. Preheat the oven to 180°C/350°F/Gas Mark 4. Grease four ramekins or moulds.

2. To make the cakes, use an electric mixer or a wooden spoon to beat the butter in a large bowl until light and fluffy, gradually add the icing sugar and whisk thoroughly. Break the sponge fingers into pieces and stir into the butter mixture together with the hazelnuts and grated chocolate. Add the egg yolks, brandy and crème de cacao and mix well.

3. Beat the egg whites until they hold stiff peaks, fold carefully into the mixture and divide evenly among the moulds. Cover with greased foil.

4. Place the moulds in a roasting tin and pour in hot water to half way up the ramekins. Carefully place in the preheated oven and bake for about 45 minutes until the mixture has set.

5. To make the sauce, put the water, sugar, orange juice and rind into a small saucepan and bring to the boil. Reduce the heat and simmer for 3 minutes. Break the chocolate into small pieces and put in a heatproof bowl set over a saucepan of gently simmering water. Melt the chocolate, stirring constantly, then slowly stir in the orange syrup.

6. Use a knife to help ease the cakes out of the moulds and turn out onto plates. Pour the sauce over and serve warm.

Makes 4

Ingredients
55 g/2 oz butter, plus extra
  for greasing
3 tbsp icing sugar
55 g/2 oz sponge fingers
25 g/1 oz ground hazelnuts
55 g/2 oz dark chocolate, grated
2 eggs, separated
1 tbsp brandy
1 tbsp crème de cacao

For the Sauce
4 tsp water
2½ tbsp caster sugar
juice and grated rind of 1 orange
125 g/4½ oz dark chocolate

Cinnamon Swirls

Makes 12

Ingredients
225 g/8 oz strong white flour
½ tsp salt
7 g/¼ oz easy-blend dried yeast
25 g/1 oz butter, cut into small
   pieces, plus extra for greasing
1 egg, lightly beaten
125 ml/4 fl oz lukewarm milk
2 tbsp maple syrup, for glazing

For the Filling
55 g/2 oz butter, softened
2 tsp ground cinnamon
50 g/1¾ oz soft light
   brown sugar
50 g/1¾ oz currants

1. Grease a baking sheet and a bowl. Sift the flour and salt into a mixing bowl and stir in the yeast.

2. Rub in the chopped butter with your fingertips until the mixture resembles breadcrumbs. Add the egg and milk and mix to form a dough.

3. Form the dough into a ball, place in the greased bowl, cover and leave to stand in a warm place for about 40 minutes, or until doubled in volume.

4. Punch down the dough lightly for 1 minute, then roll out to a rectangle measuring 30 cm x 23 cm/12 inches x 19 inches.

5. For the filling, cream together the softened butter, cinnamon and sugar until light and fluffy.

6. Spread the filling over the dough, leaving a 2.5-cm/1-inch border. Sprinkle the currants evenly over the top. Roll up the dough from one of the long edges and press down to seal.

7. Preheat the oven to 190°C/375°F/Gas Mark 5. Cut the roll into 12 slices and place them, cut side down, on the prepared baking sheet. Cover and leave to stand for 30 minutes.

8. Bake in the preheated oven for 20–30 minutes, or until the swirls are well risen.

9. Brush with maple syrup and leave to cool slightly before serving.

Cherry Tartlets

1. Preheat the oven to 190°C/375°F/Gas Mark 5. Place the flour, icing sugar, cinnamon and butter in a food processor and process until evenly blended.

2. Add the egg yolk and water to the mixture, and blend until it just binds to form a soft dough.

3. Divide the pastry into four and press into four 18-cm/4-inch loose-based tartlet tins, pressing with your knuckles to spread evenly.

4. Place on a baking sheet and bake the tartlets blind for 12–15 minutes, then remove from the oven and leave to cool. Stir the cherries into the yogurt and spoon into the cases.

5. Drizzle the tartlets with honey, sprinkle with cinnamon and serve with whole cherries.

Makes 4

Ingredients
125 g/4½ oz plain flour, sifted
2 tbsp icing sugar, sifted
½ tsp ground cinnamon
70 g/2½ oz unsalted butter,
  at room temperature
1 egg yolk
2 tbsp cold water

For the Filling
350 g/12 oz cherries, pitted
150 ml/5 fl oz Greek-style
  yogurt
2 tbsp clear honey
cinnamon and whole cherries,
  to decorate

Vanilla Whoopie Pies

Makes 12

Ingredients
250 g/9 oz plain flour
1 tsp bicarbonate of soda
large pinch of salt
175 g/6 oz butter, softened
150 g/5½ oz caster sugar
1 large egg, beaten
2 tsp vanilla extract
150 ml/5 fl oz buttermilk

For the Chocolate Buttercream Filling
115 g/4 oz milk chocolate,
  broken into pieces
115 g/4 oz unsalted butter,
  softened
250 g/9 oz icing sugar, sifted

1. Preheat the oven to 180°C/350°F/Gas Mark 4. Line two or three large baking sheets with baking paper. Sift together the plain flour, bicarbonate of soda and salt.

2. Place the butter and sugar in a large bowl and beat with an electric hand-held whisk until pale and fluffy. Beat in the egg and vanilla extract followed by half the flour mixture and then the buttermilk. Stir in the rest of the flour mixture and mix until thoroughly incorporated.

3. Pipe or spoon 24 mounds of the mixture onto the prepared baking sheets, spaced well apart to allow for spreading. Bake in the preheated oven, one sheet at a time, for 10–12 minutes, or until risen and just firm to the touch. Cool for 5 minutes then, using a palette knife, transfer to a wire rack and leave to cool completely.

4. For the filling, place the chocolate in a heatproof bowl set over a saucepan of simmering water and leave until melted. Remove from the heat and leave to cool for 20 minutes, stirring occasionally. Place the butter in a bowl and beat with an electric whisk for 2–3 minutes, or until pale and creamy. Gradually beat in the icing sugar, then beat in the chocolate.

5. To assemble, spread or pipe the buttercream on the flat side of half of the cakes. Top with the rest of the cakes.

Cinnamon Waffle Bites

1. Melt the butter in a small saucepan. Sift the flour into a bowl and gradually stir in the cream, egg yolks, spices, vanilla seeds and 2½ tablespoons of the melted butter.

2. Put the egg whites and half of the sugar in a bowl and beat until light and fluffy. Gradually add the remaining sugar and continue beating until the whipped egg white makes firm peaks. Fold a third of the egg white into the cream mixture, then mix in the rest.

3. Preheat the waffle maker and grease lightly with butter.

4. Pour a little batter into the waffle maker, spread out and cook the waffle on a medium heat until golden yellow. Continue cooking all of the waffles until the batter is used up, and place on a wire rack.

5. Brush the waffle bites with the remaining melted butter and sprinkle with sugar.

Makes 8

Ingredients
*115 g/4 oz butter, plus extra
  for greasing
100 g/3½ oz plain flour
150 ml/5 fl oz single cream
2 egg yolks
½ tsp cinnamon
pinch of ground cloves
seeds from 1 vanilla pod
3 egg whites
2 tbsp caster sugar,
  plus extra for sprinkling*

Apple Fritters

Makes 12

Ingredients

300 g/10½ oz plain flour
1½ tbsp baking powder
5 tbsp caster sugar
350 ml/12 fl oz milk
3 eggs, separated
4 apples
juice of ½ lemon
vegetable oil, for frying
icing sugar, for dusting

For the Sauce

1 vanilla pod
250 ml/9 fl oz milk
6 eggs yolks
4 tbsp caster sugar

1. Sift together the flour and baking powder into a large bowl, add the sugar, milk and egg yolks and mix to a smooth batter. Whisk the egg whites until holding firm peaks and carefully fold into the batter.

2. Peel the apples and remove the core with a corer. Cut them horizontally into ½-cm/¼-inch thick slices and rub them with the lemon juice to prevent them from browning.

3. Pour the vegetable oil into a saucepan and heat to 160°C/325°F or until a little of the batter dropped into the hot oil bubbles and rises to the surface immediately.

4. Coat the apple slices with batter, slide into the hot oil immediately, a few at a time, and fry until the apple slices are golden brown. Drain thoroughly on kitchen paper, then dust with the icing sugar and keep warm while you make the sauce.

5. To make the sauce, cut the vanilla pod in half lengthwise and scrape out the seeds. Pour the milk into a saucepan, add the vanilla seeds and the pod and bring to the boil. Meanwhile, beat the egg yolks with the sugar in a bowl until light and fluffy. Remove the vanilla pod from the hot milk and pour into the egg and sugar mixture, stirring constantly. Return to the pan and heat gently for a few minutes, stirring all the time, until just thickened. Pour into a jug and serve warm or cold with the fritters.

It's the love and care put into each batch of cakes that gives the most joy to those who eat them, and to you as the cook.

Apple Danish

1. Place the flour in a bowl and rub in 25 g/1 oz of the butter. Set aside. Dust the remaining butter with flour, grate coarsely into a bowl and chill. Stir the salt, yeast and sugar into the flour mixture.

2. In another bowl, beat the egg with the vanilla extract and water, add to the flour mixture and mix to form a dough. Knead for 10 minutes on a floured surface, then chill for 10 minutes.

3. Roll out the dough to a 30-cm x 20-cm/12-inch x 8-inch rectangle. Mark widthways into thirds and fold. Press the edges with a rolling pin and roll out to the same size as the original rectangle.

4. Sprinkle the grated butter evenly over the top two-thirds. Fold up the bottom third and fold down the top third. Press the edges, wrap in clingfilm and chill for 30 minutes. Repeat four times, chilling well each time. Chill overnight.

5. Mix together the filling ingredients. Preheat the oven to 200°C/400°F/Gas Mark 6. Grease two baking sheets.

6. Roll out the dough into a 40-cm/16-inch square and cut up to 16 squares. Pile some filling in the centre of each, reserving any juice. Brush the edges of the squares with milk and bring the corners together in the centre.

7. Place on the prepared baking sheets and chill for 15 minutes. Brush with the reserved juice and sprinkle with caster sugar.

8. Bake in the preheated oven for 10 minutes, reduce the temperature to 180°C/350°F/Gas Mark 4 and bake for a further 10–15 minutes, until browned.

9. Gently remove from the baking sheets and serve.

Makes 12–16

Ingredients
275 g/9¾ oz strong white flour, plus extra, sifted, for dusting
175 g/6 oz butter, well chilled, plus extra for greasing
½ tsp salt
7 g/¼ oz easy-blend dried yeast
2 tbsp caster sugar, plus extra for sprinkling
1 egg
1 tsp vanilla extract
6 tbsp lukewarm water
milk, for glazing

For the Filling
2 cooking apples, peeled, cored and chopped
grated rind of 1 lemon
3 tbsp sugar

Blueberry Muffins

Makes 12

Ingredients
280 g/10 oz plain flour
1 tbsp baking powder
pinch of salt
115 g/4 oz soft light
  brown sugar
150 g/5½ oz frozen blueberries
2 eggs
250 ml/9 fl oz milk
85 g/3 oz butter, melted and
  cooled
1 tsp vanilla extract
finely grated rind of 1 lemon

1. Preheat the oven to 200°C/400°F/Gas Mark 6. Place 12 paper cases in a muffin tin. Sift together the flour, baking powder and salt into a large bowl. Stir in the sugar and blueberries.

2. Lightly beat the eggs in a large jug, then beat in the milk, melted butter, vanilla extract and lemon rind. Make a well in the centre of the dry ingredients and pour in the beaten liquid ingredients. Stir gently until just combined; do not over-mix.

3. Divide the mixture evenly between the paper cases. Bake in the preheated oven for about 20 minutes, or until well risen, golden brown and firm to the touch.

4. Leave the muffins in the tin for 5 minutes, then serve warm or transfer to a wire rack and leave to cool.

Chocolate & Orange Muffins

1. Preheat the oven to 200°C/400°F/Gas Mark 6. Place 12 paper cases in a muffin tin.

2. Finely grate the rind from the oranges and squeeze the juice. Add enough milk to make up the juice to 250 ml/9 fl oz, then add the orange rind. Sift together the flour, cocoa, baking powder and salt into a large bowl. Stir in the brown sugar and chocolate chips. Place the eggs in a large jug or bowl and beat lightly, then beat in the milk and orange mixture and the oil. Make a well in the centre of the dry ingredients and pour in the beaten liquid ingredients. Stir gently until just combined; do not over-mix. Divide the mixture evenly between the paper cases.

3. Bake in the preheated oven for 20 minutes, or until well risen and firm to the touch. Leave to cool in the tin for 5 minutes, then transfer to a wire rack to cool completely.

4. To make the icing, place the chocolate in a heatproof bowl, add the butter and water, then set the bowl over a saucepan of gently simmering water and heat, stirring, until melted. Remove from the heat and sift in the icing sugar. Beat until smooth, then spread the icing on top of the muffins and decorate with strips of orange zest.

Makes 12

Ingredients
2 oranges
about 125 ml/4 fl oz milk
225 g/8 oz plain flour
55 g/2 oz cocoa powder
1 tbsp baking powder
pinch of salt
115 g/4 oz soft light brown
  sugar
150 g/5½ oz plain
  chocolate chips
2 eggs
6 tbsp sunflower oil or 85 g/
  3 oz butter, melted and cooled
strips of orange zest,
  to decorate

For the Icing
55 g/2 oz plain chocolate,
  broken into pieces
25 g/1 oz butter
2 tbsp water
175 g/6 oz icing sugar

Blueberry Profiteroles

Makes 12

Ingredients
125 ml/4 fl oz milk
55 g/2 oz butter
125 g/4½ oz plain flour
pinch of salt
3 eggs, beaten

For the Filling
300 ml/10 fl oz double cream
280 g/10 oz blueberries
25 g/1 oz caster sugar
1 tsp lemon juice
55 g/2 oz blackberries
icing sugar, for dusting

1. Preheat the oven to 200°C/400°F/Gas Mark 6. Line a baking sheet with baking paper.

2. To make the pastry, put the milk and butter into a medium saucepan and bring to the boil. Add the flour and salt and with a wooden spoon beat thoroughly until a smooth ball of dough has formed. Leave to cool for 10–15 minutes.

3. Use a wooden spoon to beat the beaten eggs, a little at a time, into the dough (it may not all be needed) to form a smooth, glossy paste. Spoon the dough into a piping bag fitted with a large star-shaped nozzle and pipe 12 balls (5 cm/2 inches in diameter) onto the prepared baking sheet. Bake in the preheated oven for about 20–25 minutes. Place a baking sheet sprinkled with hot water on the floor of the oven to help the profiteroles rise better. Leave the profiteroles to cool and cut in half horizontally.

4. To make the filling, whip the cream until holding stiff peaks. Process 225 g/8 oz blueberries with the caster sugar and lemon juice and gently fold into the cream. Spoon the cream filling into a piping bag with a large nozzle and pipe onto the lower halves of the profiteroles. Sprinkle the remaining blueberries and the blackberries on top. Put the top halves into position and dust with the icing sugar to serve.

Cinnamon Orange Fritters

1. Sift the flour into a bowl and stir in the yeast and sugar.

2. Add the milk, egg, orange rind, flower water and butter and mix to a soft dough, kneading until smooth.

3. Cover and leave in a warm place until doubled in volume. Roll out on a lightly floured surface to a thickness of 1 cm/½ inch, and cut into eight 7.5-cm/3-inch squares.

4. Heat the oil to 180°C/350°F. Fry the fritters in batches until golden brown. Remove with a slotted spoon and drain on kitchen paper.

5. Sprinkle with cinnamon sugar and serve hot with orange slices or segments.

Makes 8

Ingredients
250 g/9 oz plain flour
1 tsp easy-blend dried yeast
1½ tbsp caster sugar
125 ml/4 fl oz lukewarm milk
1 egg, beaten
finely grated rind of
* 1 small orange*
1 tsp orange flower water
40 g/1½ oz butter, melted
sunflower oil, for deep frying
cinnamon sugar, for dusting
orange slices or segments,
* to serve*

Summer Fruit Tartlets

Makes 12

Ingredients

200 g/7 oz plain flour,
  plus extra for dusting
85 g/3 oz icing sugar, sifted
55 g/2 oz ground almonds
115 g/4 oz butter
1 egg yolk
1 tbsp milk
350 g/12 oz fresh summer
  berries, including
  strawberries

For the Filling

225 g/8 oz cream cheese
icing sugar, to taste, plus extra,
  sifted, for dusting

1. Sift the flour and icing sugar into a bowl. Stir in the almonds. Add the butter, rubbing in until the mixture resembles breadcrumbs. Add the egg yolk and milk and work in until the dough binds together. Wrap in clingfilm and chill for 30 minutes.

2. Preheat the oven to 200°C/400°F/Gas Mark 6. Roll out the dough on a lightly floured surface and use it to line 12 deep tartlet tins. Prick the bases and press a piece of foil into each.

3. Bake in the preheated oven for 10–15 minutes, or until light golden brown. Remove the foil and bake for a further 2–3 minutes. Transfer to a wire rack to cool.

4. Halve the strawberries. For the filling, place the cream cheese and icing sugar in a bowl and mix together. Place a spoonful of filling in each tartlet and arrange the berries on top.

5. Dust with sifted icing sugar and serve immediately.

Sugar Cookies

1. Place the butter and sugar in a bowl and beat together until pale and creamy. Beat in the lemon rind and egg yolk. Sift in the flour and mix to a soft dough. Turn out onto a floured work surface and knead until smooth, adding a little more flour, if necessary. Halve the dough, shape into balls, wrap in clingfilm and chill in the refrigerator for 1 hour.

2. Preheat the oven to 180°C/350°F/Gas Mark 4. Lightly grease two large baking sheets.

3. Roll out the dough on a lightly floured work surface to a thickness of 5 mm/¼ inch. Using 7-cm/2¾-inch flower-shaped and heart-shaped cutters stamp out 20 cookies, re-rolling the dough as necessary. Place on the prepared baking sheets and sprinkle with sugar.

4. Bake in the preheated oven for 10–12 minutes, or until pale golden. Leave to cool on the baking sheets for 2–3 minutes, then transfer to a wire rack to cool completely.

Makes 20

Ingredients
115 g/4 oz butter, softened,
*   plus extra for greasing*
55 g/2 oz caster sugar,
*   plus extra for sprinkling*
1 tsp finely grated lemon rind
1 egg yolk
175 g/6 oz plain flour,
*   plus extra for dusting*

Chocolate Chip Cookies

Makes 8

Ingredients

unsalted butter, melted,
  for greasing
175 g/6 oz plain flour, sifted
1 tsp baking powder
125. g/4½ oz margarine, melted
85 g/3 oz light muscovado
  sugar
55 g/2 oz caster sugar
½ tsp vanilla extract
1 egg, beaten
125 g/4½ oz plain chocolate
  chips

1. Preheat the oven to 190°C/375°F/Gas Mark 5. Lightly grease two baking sheets.

2. Place all of the ingredients in a large mixing bowl and beat until well combined.

3. Place tablespoons of the mixture on the prepared baking sheets, spaced well apart.

4. Bake in the preheated oven for 10–12 minutes, or until golden brown. Transfer to a wire rack and leave to cool.

Snickerdoodles

1. Preheat the oven to 180°C/350°F/Gas Mark 4. Line two large baking sheets with baking paper.

2. Put the butter and caster sugar into a bowl and beat together until pale and creamy. Gradually beat in the egg and vanilla extract. Sift together the flour and baking powder and stir into the bowl. Mix to a smooth dough.

3. Mix together the granulated sugar and cinnamon on a plate. Divide the dough into 24 even-sized pieces and shape each piece into a walnut-sized ball. Roll the balls in the cinnamon sugar, then place on the prepared baking sheets, spaced well apart to allow for spreading. Flatten each ball slightly with your fingers.

4. Bake in the preheated oven for 12–14 minutes, or until golden. Leave to cool on the baking sheets for 5 minutes, then transfer to a wire rack to cool completely.

Makes 24

Ingredients
85 g/3 oz butter, softened
175 g/6 oz caster sugar
1 large egg, beaten
½ tsp vanilla extract
250 g/9 oz plain flour
1 tsp baking powder
3 tbsp granulated sugar
1 tbsp ground cinnamon

Marzipan Ring Cookies

Makes 8

Ingredients

125 g/4½ oz unsalted butter,
  softened
30 g/1 oz caster sugar
½ tsp almond essence
125 g/4½ oz plain flour, sieved
1 tbsp milk, to mix
40 g/1½ oz marzipan
4 tsp apricot jam, warmed
icing sugar, sifted, for dusting

1. Preheat the oven to 190°C/375°F/Gas Mark 5. Place 8 paper cases in a shallow bun tin.

2. Place the butter, caster sugar and almond essence in a food processor and process until pale and fluffy. Add the flour and process to a soft dough, adding milk if necessary. Spoon the mixture into a piping bag fitted with a large star-shaped nozzle. Pipe the mixture in a spiral around the sides of each case, leaving a dip in the centre. Cut the marzipan into 8 cubes and press one into the centre of each cookie.

3. Bake in the preheated oven for 15–20 minutes, until pale and golden. Lift the cakes onto a wire rack to cool. Once the cakes have cooled, spoon a little of the apricot jam into the centre of each. Dust the cookies with icing sugar, and serve.

Crown Loaf

1. Grease a baking tray. Sift the flour and salt into a bowl. Stir in the yeast. Rub in the diced butter with your fingertips. Add the milk and egg and mix to form a dough.

2. Place the dough in a greased bowl, cover and leave in a warm place for 40 minutes, or until doubled in volume.

3. Punch down lightly for 1 minute. Roll out to a 30-cm x 23-cm/ 12-inch x 9-inch rectangle.

4. For the filling, cream the butter and sugar until light and fluffy. Stir in the hazelnuts, ginger, mixed peel and rum.

5. Spread the filling over the dough, leaving a 2.5-cm/1-inch border.

6. Roll up the dough, starting from one of the long edges, into a sausage shape. Cut into slices at 5-cm/2-inch intervals and place in a circle on the prepared baking tray with the slices just touching.

7. Cover and leave in a warm place for 30 minutes. Meanwhile, preheat the oven to 190°C/375°F/Gas Mark 5. Bake the loaf in the preheated oven for 20–30 minutes, or until golden.

8. For the icing, mix the sugar with enough lemon juice to form a thin icing. Leave the loaf to cool slightly before drizzling with the icing. Allow the icing to set before serving.

Serves 9

Ingredients
225 g/8 oz strong white flour
½ tsp salt
7 g/¼ oz easy-blend dried yeast
2 tbsp butter, diced, plus extra
  for greasing
125 ml/4 fl oz lukewarm milk
1 egg, lightly beaten

For the Filling
4 tbsp butter, softened
50 g/1¾ oz soft light
  brown sugar
2 tbsp chopped hazelnuts
1 tbsp crystallized ginger
50 g/1¾ oz chopped mixed peel
1 tbsp dark rum or brandy

For the Icing
115 g/4 oz icing sugar, sifted
1–2 tbsp lemon juice

Poppy Seed Plait

Makes 1 loaf

Ingredients

225 g/8 oz strong white flour,
* plus extra for dusting*
1 tsp salt
2 tbsp skimmed milk powder
1½ tbsp caster sugar
1 tsp easy-blend dried yeast
175 ml/6 fl oz lukewarm water
2 tbsp vegetable oil, plus extra
* for greasing*
5 tbsp poppy seeds

For the Topping

1 egg yolk
1 tbsp milk
1 tbsp caster sugar
2 tbsp poppy seeds

1. Sift the flour and salt together into a bowl and stir in the milk powder, sugar and yeast. Make a well in the centre, pour in the water and oil and stir until the dough begins to come together.

2. Add the poppy seeds and knead until fully combined and the dough leaves the side of the bowl. Turn out onto a lightly floured surface and knead well for about 10 minutes, until smooth and elastic.

3. Brush a bowl with oil. Shape the dough into a ball, put it in the bowl, cover and leave to rise in a warm place for 1 hour, or until doubled in volume.

4. Oil a baking sheet. Turn out the dough onto a lightly floured surface, knock back and knead for 1–2 minutes. Divide into three equal pieces and shape each into a rope 25–30 cm/10–12 inches long.

5. Place the ropes side by side and press together at one end. Plait the dough, pinch the other end together and tuck underneath.

6. Put the loaf on the prepared baking sheet, cover and leave to rise in a warm place for 30 minutes. Meanwhile, preheat the oven to 200°C/400°F/Gas Mark 6.

7. For the topping, beat the egg yolk with the milk and sugar. Brush the egg glaze over the top of the loaf and sprinkle with the poppy seeds.

8. Bake in the preheated oven for 30–35 minutes, until golden brown. Transfer to a wire rack and leave to cool.

9. Serve plain or toasted as a lunchtime treat.

Wholemeal Loaf

1. Place the flour, milk powder, salt, sugar and yeast in a large bowl. Pour in the oil and add the water, then mix well to make a smooth dough.

2. Turn out onto a lightly floured surface and knead well for about 10 minutes, or until smooth. Brush a bowl with oil. Shape the dough into a ball, place it in the bowl and cover with a damp tea towel. Leave to rise in a warm place for 1 hour, or until the dough has doubled in volume.

3. Preheat the oven to 220°C/425°F/Gas Mark 7. Oil a 900-g/ 2-lb loaf tin. Turn the dough out onto a lightly floured surface and knead for 1 minute, or until smooth. Shape the dough the length of the tin and three times the width. Fold the dough into three widthways and place it in the tin with the join underneath. Cover and leave in a warm place for 30 minutes, or until it has risen above the tin.

4. Place in the preheated oven and bake for 30 minutes, or until firm and golden brown. Test that the loaf is cooked by tapping on the base with your knuckles – it should sound hollow. Transfer to a wire rack to cool.

Makes 1 loaf

Ingredients:
225 g/8 oz strong wholemeal flour, plus extra for dusting
1 tbsp skimmed milk powder
1 tsp salt
2 tbsp soft light brown sugar
1 tsp easy-blend dried yeast
1½ tbsp sunflower oil, plus extra for greasing
175 ml/6 fl oz lukewarm water

White Crusty Loaf

Makes 1 loaf

Ingredients
1 egg
1 egg yolk
*150–200 ml/5–7 fl oz lukewarm
   water*
*500 g/1 lb 2 oz strong white
   flour, sifted, plus extra
   for dusting*
1½ tsp salt
2 tsp sugar
1 tsp easy-blend dried yeast
25 g/1 oz butter, diced
oil, for greasing

1. Place the egg and egg yolk in a jug and beat lightly to mix. Add enough water to make up to 300 ml/10 fl oz. Stir well.

2. Place the flour, salt, sugar and yeast in a large bowl. Add the butter and rub it in with your fingertips until the mixture resembles fine breadcrumbs.

3. Make a well in the centre, add the egg mixture and work to a smooth dough. Turn out onto a lightly floured surface and knead well for about 10 minutes, until smooth.

4. Brush a bowl with oil. Shape the dough into a ball, place in the bowl, cover and leave to rise in a warm place for 1 hour, or until doubled in volume.

5. Preheat the oven to 220°C/425°F/Gas Mark 7. Oil a 900-g/2-lb loaf tin. Turn out the dough onto a lightly floured surface and knead for 1 minute until smooth.

6. Shape the dough so it is the same length as the loaf tin and three times the width. Fold the dough in three widthways and place it in the tin with the join underneath.

7. Cover and leave in a warm place for 30 minutes, until the dough has risen above the tin.

8. Place in the preheated oven and bake for 30 minutes, or until firm and golden brown. Transfer to a wire rack and leave to cool.

9. Cut into thick slices and serve.

Mixed Seed Bread

1. Place the flours, milk powder, salt, sugar and yeast in a large bowl. Pour in the oil and add the lemon juice and water. Stir in the seeds and mix well to make a smooth dough. Turn out onto a lightly floured surface and knead well for about 10 minutes, until smooth.

2. Brush a bowl with oil. Shape the dough into a ball, place it in the bowl and cover with a damp tea towel. Leave to rise in a warm place for 1 hour, until the dough has doubled in volume. Oil a 900-g/2-lb loaf tin. Turn out the dough onto a lightly floured surface and knead for 1 minute until smooth. Shape the dough the length of the tin and three times the width. Fold the dough in three widthways and place it in the tin with the join underneath. Cover and leave in a warm place for 30 minutes, until it has risen above the tin.

3. Preheat the oven to 220°C/425°F/Gas Mark 7. For the topping, lightly beat the egg white with the water to make a glaze. Just before baking, brush the glaze over the loaf, then gently press the sunflower seeds all over the top.

4. Bake in the preheated oven for 30 minutes, or until firm and golden brown. Test that the loaf is cooked by tapping on the base with your knuckles – it should sound hollow. Transfer to a wire rack to cool.

Makes 1 loaf

Ingredients
375 g/13 oz strong white flour,
* plus extra for dusting*
125 g/4½ oz rye flour
1½ tbsp skimmed milk powder
1½ tsp salt
1 tbsp soft light brown sugar
1 tsp easy-blend dried yeast
1½ tbsp sunflower oil,
* plus extra for greasing*
2 tsp lemon juice
300 ml/10 fl oz lukewarm water
1 tsp caraway seeds
½ tsp poppy seeds
½ tsp sesame seeds

For the Topping
1 egg white
1 tbsp water
1 tbsp sunflower seeds
* or pumpkin seeds*

Rye Bread

Makes 1 loaf

Ingredients

450 g/1 lb rye flour
225 g/8 oz strong white flour,
 plus extra for dusting
2 tsp salt
2 tsp soft light brown sugar
1½ tsp easy-blend dried yeast
425 ml/15 fl oz lukewarm water
2 tsp vegetable oil, plus extra
 for greasing
1 egg white

1. Sift the flours and salt together into a bowl. Add the sugar and yeast and stir to mix. Make a well in the centre and pour in the water and oil.

2. Stir until the dough begins to come together, then knead until it leaves the side of the bowl. Turn out onto a lightly floured surface and knead for 10 minutes, until elastic and smooth.

3. Brush a bowl with oil. Shape the dough into a ball, put it in the bowl, cover and leave to rise in a warm place for 2 hours, or until doubled in volume.

4. Oil a baking tray. Turn out the dough onto a lightly floured surface and knock back, then knead for 10 minutes.

5. Shape the dough into a ball, put it on the prepared baking tray and cover. Leave to rise in a warm place for a further 40 minutes, or until doubled in volume.

6. Meanwhile, preheat the oven to 190°C/375°F/Gas Mark 5. Beat the egg white with 1 tablespoon of water in a bowl.

7. Bake the loaf in the preheated oven for 20 minutes, then remove from the oven and brush the top with the egg white glaze. Return to the oven and bake for a further 20 minutes.

8. Brush the top of the loaf with the glaze again and return to the oven for a further 20–30 minutes, until the crust is a rich brown colour. Transfer to a wire rack to cool.

9. Serve with good-quality butter or a topping of your choice.

Christmas Treats

Stollen

Makes 1 stollen

Ingredients
150 ml/5 fl oz lukewarm milk
50 g/1¾ oz caster sugar
2 tsp dried active yeast
350 g/12 oz strong plain flour,
*   plus extra for dusting*
½ tsp salt
125 g/4½ oz softened butter,
*   plus extra for greasing*
1 egg, beaten
50 g/1¾ oz currants
50 g/1¾ oz sultanas
50 g/1¾ oz candied lemon peel
50 g/1¾ oz glacé cherries
25 g/1 oz chopped almonds
grated rind of ½ lemon
175 g/6 oz marzipan
icing sugar, for dusting

1. To make the stollen dough, put the milk and one teaspoon of the sugar in a bowl, sprinkle in the yeast and stir, or follow packet instructions. Leave in a warm place until frothy.

2. Sift the flour and salt into a bowl and add the remaining sugar. Make a well in the centre. Pour in the yeast mixture. Add the butter and egg and mix to a smooth dough. Knead for 5–6 minutes until smooth and elastic.

3. Knead the currants, sultanas, lemon peel, cherries, almonds and lemon rind into the dough. Cover the bowl and leave to rise in a warm place for 2 hours until the dough has doubled in volume.

4. Turn the dough out onto a floured surface and knead for 2–3 minutes. Break up the marzipan or cut it into small pieces and knead into the dough.

5. Roll the dough into a cylinder shape. Grease a baking sheet and place the stollen on it. Cover with a cloth and leave to rise again until it has doubled in volume. Preheat the oven to 190°C/375°F/Gas Mark 5.

6. Bake the stollen for about 40 minutes or until golden. Place on a wire rack and leave to cool completely. Dust with plenty of icing sugar to serve.

Lebkuchen

1. Preheat the oven to 180°C/350°F/Gas Mark 4. Line several baking trays with baking paper.

2. Put the eggs and sugar in a heatproof bowl set over a saucepan of gently simmering water. Whisk until thick and foamy. Remove the bowl from the saucepan and continue to whisk for 2 minutes.

3. Sift the flour, cocoa powder, cinnamon, cardamom, cloves and nutmeg into the bowl and stir in with the ground almonds and mixed peel. Drop heaped teaspoonfuls of the mixture onto the prepared baking trays, spreading them gently into smooth mounds.

4. Bake in the preheated oven for 15–20 minutes, until light brown and slightly soft to the touch. Cool on the baking trays for 10 minutes, then transfer to wire racks to cool completely.

5. Put the plain and white chocolate in two separate heatproof bowls set over two saucepans of gently simmering water until melted. Dip half the biscuits in the melted plain chocolate and half in the white chocolate. Sprinkle with sugar crystals and leave to set.

Makes 60

Ingredients
3 eggs
200 g/7 oz golden caster sugar
55 g/2 oz plain flour
2 tsp cocoa powder
1 tsp ground cinnamon
½ tsp ground cardamom
¼ tsp ground cloves
¼ tsp ground nutmeg
175 g/6 oz ground almonds
55 g/2 oz chopped mixed peel

For the Decoration
115 g/4 oz plain chocolate
115 g/4 oz white chocolate
sugar crystals

Spicy Citrus Cookies

Makes 65

Ingredients
2 eggs
250 g/9 oz caster sugar
pinch of salt
70 g/2½ oz candied orange
 peel, finely chopped
grated rind of ½ lemon
300 g/10½ oz plain flour,
 plus extra for dusting
2 tbsp ground mixed spice
½ tsp baking powder
1 tbsp water

1. To make the dough, put the eggs, sugar and salt in a bowl and beat with a balloon whisk until light and frothy. In a separate bowl mix the orange peel, lemon rind, flour and half of the mixed spice together.

2. Dissolve the baking powder in the water and stir into the egg mixture then gradually fold the flour mixture to make a firm dough. Cover and chill in the refrigerator for 3–4 hours or overnight.

3. Preheat the oven to 200°C/400°F/Gas Mark 6. Line two large baking trays with baking paper.

4. Turn the biscuit dough out onto a floured surface. Knead gently until smooth then, using floured hands, divide and shape into about 65 small balls. Flatten each ball slightly.

5. Place the flattened dough balls on the baking trays and sprinkle with the remaining mixed spice.

6. Bake in the preheated oven for 10–12 minutes until crisp. Leave on the trays for 5 minutes then transfer to a wire cooling rack and leave to cool completely.

Snowflake Gingerbread

1. Preheat the oven to 180°C/350°F/Gas Mark 4. Grease three baking sheets.

2. Sift the flour, ginger and bicarbonate of soda together in a bowl. Add the butter and rub into the flour until the mixture resembles fine breadcrumbs, then stir in the brown sugar.

3. In another bowl, beat together the egg and golden syrup with a fork. Pour this mixture into the flour mixture and mix to make a smooth dough, kneading lightly with your hands.

4. Roll the dough out on a lightly floured work surface to about 5 mm/¼ inch thick and cut into shapes using a snowflake-shaped cutter. Transfer the cookies to the prepared baking sheets.

5. Bake in the preheated oven for 10 minutes until golden brown. Remove the cookies from the oven and allow to cool for 5 minutes before transferring, using a palette knife, to a wire rack to cool completely.

6. Once the cookies are cool, mix together the icing sugar and lemon juice until smooth and place into a piping bag fitted with a very small nozzle. Pipe snowflake shapes onto each biscuit, using the icing. Leave to set for a few hours.

Makes 30

Ingredients
350 g/12 oz plain flour,
   plus extra for dusting
1 tbsp ground ginger
1 tsp bicarbonate of soda
100 g/3½ oz butter, softened,
   plus extra for greasing
175 g/6 oz soft brown sugar
1 egg, beaten
4 tbsp golden syrup

For the Decoration
115 g/4 oz icing sugar
2 tbsp lemon juice

Cookie Candy Canes

Makes 40

Ingredients

350 g/12 oz plain flour,
  plus extra for dusting
1 tsp bicarbonate of soda
100 g/3½ oz butter, softened,
  plus extra for greasing
175 g/6 oz soft brown sugar
1 egg, beaten
1 tsp vanilla extract
4 tbsp golden syrup

For the Decoration

450 g/1 lb icing sugar
135 ml/4½ fl oz lemon juice
glycerine-based red food
  colouring

1. Preheat the oven to 180°C/350°F/Gas Mark 4. Grease three baking sheets.

2. Sift the flour and bicarbonate of soda together in a bowl. Add the butter and rub into the flour mixture and resembles fine breadcrumbs, then stir in the brown sugar. In another bowl, beat together the egg, vanilla extract and golden syrup with a fork. Pour this mixture into the flour blend and stir to make a smooth dough, kneading lightly with your hands.

3. Roll the dough out on a lightly floured work surface to about 5 mm/¼ inch thick and cut into shapes using a candy cane-shaped cutter. Transfer the cookies to the prepared baking sheets. Bake in the preheated oven for 10 minutes, until golden brown. Remove the cookies from the oven and allow to cool for 5 minutes, before transferring, using a palette knife, to a wire rack to cool completely.

4. Once the cookies are cool, mix together 280 g/10 oz of the icing sugar and 75 ml/2½ fl oz of the lemon juice until smooth. Spoon the mixture into a piping bag fitted with a very fine nozzle and pipe the icing around the edge of the cookies. Empty any remaining icing into a small bowl, colour it with the red food colouring and cover with clingfilm. Mix the remaining icing sugar with the remaining lemon juice until smooth and runny. Spoon this into the centre of each cookie and encourage it to the piped edge to flood each biscuit. Allow to set overnight. Spoon the red icing into a piping bag fitted with a very fine nozzle and pipe stripes, dots and swirls over the dry iced cookies.

Chocolate Covered Gingerbread

1. Place the butter, sugar and golden syrup in a saucepan and heat gently, stirring all the time, until the butter has melted and the sugar has dissolved. Leave to cool for 10 minutes.

2. Sift the flour, ginger, mixed spice and bicarbonate of soda into a large bowl. Make a well in the centre and pour in the melted mixture and beaten egg. Mix to a soft dough. Knead lightly until smooth then wrap in clingfilm and chill in the refrigerator for 30 minutes.

3. Preheat the oven to 180°C/350°F/Gas Mark 4. Grease two large baking sheets.

4. Roll the dough out on a lightly floured surface to a 5-mm/¼-inch thickness. Using a 7-cm/2¾-inch round cookie cutter, stamp out 18 rounds, re-kneading and re-rolling the dough as necessary. Place on the prepared baking sheets.

5. Bake in the preheated oven for 10 minutes, or until golden and just set. Leave on the baking sheets for 2–3 minutes then transfer to a wire rack to cool completely.

6. To decorate, dip the top of each gingerbread cookie in the melted plain chocolate to completely cover, then place on a wire rack. Spoon the melted milk chocolate into a paper piping bag. Snip the end and pipe swirls or zig-zags over the chocolate-coated cookies. Leave in a cool place until the chocolate has set.

Makes 18

Ingredients

85 g/3 oz butter, diced,
  plus extra for greasing
115 g/4 oz light muscovado
  sugar
2 tbsp golden syrup
275 g/9 ¾ oz plain flour,
  plus extra for dusting
2 tsp ground ginger
½ tsp mixed spice
1 tsp bicarbonate of soda
1 egg, lightly beaten
250 g/9 oz dark chocolate,
  melted
55 g/2 oz milk chocolate,
  melted

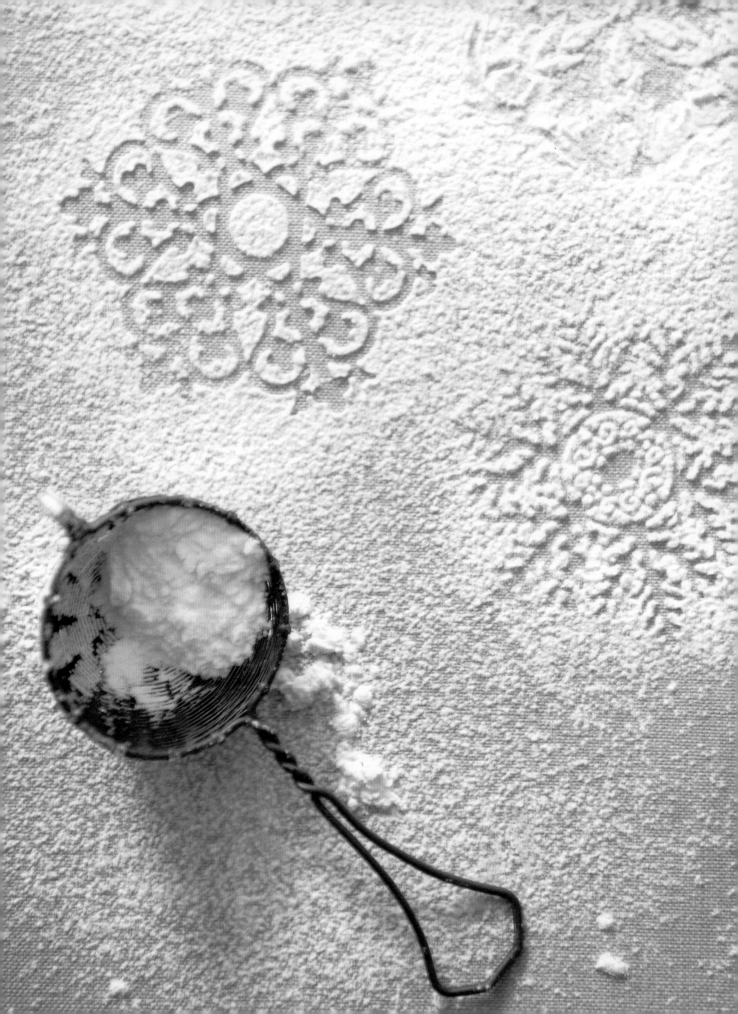

Cinnamon Stars

Makes 28

Ingredients
2 egg whites
175 g/6 oz caster sugar
2 tsp ground cinnamon
175 g/6 oz roasted chopped
  hazelnuts, coarsely ground
175 g/6 oz ground almonds
25 g/1 oz icing sugar, plus extra
  for dusting

For the Icing
1 egg white
200 g/7 oz icing sugar, sifted
1–2 tsp lemon juice

1. Place the egg whites in a large bowl and, using a hand-held electric mixer, whisk until holding soft peaks. Gradually whisk in the caster sugar to make a firm glossy meringue mixture.

2. Fold in the cinnamon, ground hazelnuts and almonds to make a firm, slightly sticky dough. Cover and chill in the refrigerator for 1 hour.

3. Preheat the oven to 150°C/300°F/Gas Mark 2. Line two large baking sheets with baking paper.

4. Sift half the icing sugar onto a work surface. Add the dough and knead lightly until no longer sticky, sifting over more icing sugar if necessary.

5. Dust a rolling pin thickly with icing sugar and roll the dough out to 1-cm/½-inch thickness. Using a small star-shaped cutter (about 6-cm/2½-inch) stamp out stars and place on the prepared baking sheets. Re-roll the dough as necessary, adding more icing sugar to prevent it from sticking.

6. To make the icing, whisk the egg white in a bowl and gradually whisk in the icing sugar until stiff. Whisk in enough of the lemon juice to give a spreadable consistency. Using a small palette knife, gently spread a little of the icing onto the top of each star.

7. Bake in the preheated oven for 15–20 minutes until just set. Turn the oven off and leave the door ajar. Leave the baking trays in the oven for 30 minutes. Transfer to a wire rack and leave to cool completely. Dust lightly with icing sugar.

Christmas Tree Cookies

1. Sift the flour and spices into a bowl and rub in the butter until the mixture resembles breadcrumbs. Add the honey and mix together well to form a soft dough. Wrap the dough in clingfilm and chill in the refrigerator for 30 minutes.

2. Meanwhile, preheat the oven to 180°C/350°F/Gas Mark 4 and grease two baking sheets. Divide the dough in half. Roll out one piece of dough on a floured work surface to about 5 mm/¼ inch thick. Cut out tree shapes using a cutter or cardboard template. Repeat with the remaining piece of dough.

3. Put the cookies on the prepared baking sheets and, using a skewer, make a hole through the top of each biscuit large enough to thread a ribbon through. Chill in the refrigerator for 15 minutes.

4. Bake in the preheated oven for 10–12 minutes, until golden. Leave to cool on the baking sheets for 5 minutes, then transfer to a wire rack to cool completely. Decorate the trees with white icing and coloured balls, then thread a length of ribbon through each hole and knot. Hang from the Christmas tree.

Makes 12

Ingredients
150 g/5½ oz plain flour,
  plus extra for dusting
1 tsp ground cinnamon
½ tsp ground nutmeg
½ tsp ground ginger
70 g/2½ oz unsalted butter,
  softened, plus extra
  for greasing
3 tbsp honey

For the Decoration
white icing
edible coloured balls

Chocolate Dominos

Makes 16

Ingredients
175 g/6 oz self-raising flour
25 g/1 oz ground almonds
175 g/6 oz caster sugar
175 g/6 oz butter, softened,
  plus extra for greasing
3 large eggs, lightly beaten
½ tsp almond extract
2 tbsp seedless raspberry jam
200 g/7 oz marzipan
icing sugar, for dusting

**For the Chocolate Glaze &
Decoration**
175 g/6 oz dark chocolate,
  broken into pieces
50 g/1¾ oz unsalted butter
2 tbsp golden syrup
40 g/1 ½ oz white chocolate,
  melted

1. Preheat the oven to 180°C/350°F/Gas Mark 4. Grease a 20-cm/8-inch square cake tin and line the base with baking paper.

2. Sift the flour into a large bowl and add the ground almonds, caster sugar, butter, eggs and almond extract. Beat with an electric handheld whisk for 2–3 minutes until thoroughly combined. Spoon the mixture into the prepared cake tin and gently level the surface. Bake in the preheated oven for 35–40 minutes, or until golden, risen and just firm to the touch. Leave in the tin for 10 minutes then turn out onto a wire rack and leave to cool completely.

3. Place the cake on a board and, using a serrated knife, level the top of the cake, then spread with jam. Roll out the marzipan thinly on a surface lightly dusted with icing sugar and trim to a 20-cm/8-inch square. Gently place the square of marzipan on top of the cake and smooth flat with your hands. Cut the cake into 16 smaller square cakes. Place all the cakes on a board and put in the freezer for about 45 minutes until just firm.

4. To make the chocolate glaze, place the dark chocolate, butter and syrup in a heatproof bowl set over a pan of simmering water. Leave until melted then remove from the heat and stir until smooth. Leave in a cool place for 30–40 minutes, stirring occasionally until the glaze has thickened but still has a spoonable consistency.

5. Remove the cakes from the freezer. Push the prongs of a fork into the base of one cake and, holding it over the bowl, spoon the chocolate glaze liberally over the cake to coat the top and sides. Allow the excess glaze to run back into the bowl. Carefully place on a wire rack. Repeat to coat the rest of the cakes with the glaze. Spoon the melted white chocolate into a paper piping bag and snip off the end with scissors. Pipe dots on the cakes to decorate. Leave in a cool place until set.

Spiced Rum Cookies

Ingredients

- 175 g/6 oz unsalted butter, softened, plus extra for greasing
- 175 g/6 oz dark muscovado sugar
- 225 g/8 oz plain flour
- pinch of salt
- ½ tsp bicarbonate of soda
- 1 tsp ground cinnamon
- ¼ tsp ground coriander
- ½ tsp ground nutmeg
- ¼ tsp ground cloves
- 2 tbsp dark rum

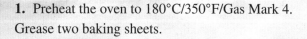

1. Preheat the oven to 180°C/350°F/Gas Mark 4. Grease two baking sheets.

2. Cream together the butter and sugar and whisk until light and fluffy. Sift together the flour, salt, bicarbonate of soda, cinnamon, coriander, nutmeg and cloves into the creamed mixture.

3. Stir the dark rum into the creamed mixture. Place 18 spoonfuls of the dough onto the prepared baking sheets, spaced well apart. Flatten each one slightly with the back of a spoon.

4. Bake in a preheated oven for 10–12 minutes until golden. Leave the cookies to cool and crisp on wire racks before serving.

Cranberry & Coconut Cookies

Makes about 30

Ingredients

- 225 g/8 oz butter, softened
- 140 g/5 oz caster sugar
- 1 egg yolk, lightly beaten
- 2 tsp vanilla extract
- 280 g/10 oz plain flour
- pinch of salt
- 40 g/1½ oz desiccated coconut
- 60 g/2¼ oz dried cranberries

1. Preheat the oven to 190°C/375°F/Gas Mark 5. Line two baking sheets with baking paper.

2. Put the butter and sugar into a bowl and mix well with a wooden spoon, then beat in the egg yolk and vanilla extract. Sift together the flour and salt into the mixture, add the coconut and cranberries and stir until thoroughly combined. Scoop up tablespoons of the dough and place in mounds on the prepared baking sheets, spaced well apart.

3. Bake in the preheated oven for 12–15 minutes, until golden brown. Leave to cool on the baking sheets for 5–10 minutes, then, using a palette knife, carefully transfer to wire racks to cool completely.

Christmas Macaroons

1. Place the ground almonds, icing sugar and mixed spice in a food processor and process for 15 seconds. Sift the mixture into a bowl. Line two baking sheets with greaseproof paper.

2. Place the egg whites in a large bowl and whisk until they hold soft peaks. Gradually whisk in the caster sugar to make a firm, glossy meringue. Using a spatula, fold the almond mixture into the meringue one third at a time. When all the dry ingredients are thoroughly incorporated, continue to cut and fold the mixture until it forms a shiny batter with a thick, ribbon-like consistency.

3. Pour the mixture into a piping bag fitted with a 1-cm/½-inch plain nozzle. Pipe 32 small rounds onto the prepared baking sheets. Tap the baking sheets firmly onto a work surface to remove air bubbles. Sprinkle half the macaroons with the grated nutmeg and gold dragées. Leave at room temperature for 30 minutes. Meanwhile, preheat the oven to 160°C/325°F/Gas Mark 3.

4. Bake in the preheated oven for 10–15 minutes. Cool for 10 minutes, then carefully peel the macaroons off the greaseproof paper. Leave to cool completely.

5. To make the filling, beat the butter and orange juice and rind in a bowl until fluffy. Gradually beat in the mixed spice and icing sugar until smooth and creamy. Fold in the glacé cherries. Use to sandwich pairs of macaroons together.

Makes 16

Ingredients
70 g/2¾ oz ground almonds
115 g/4 oz icing sugar
1 tsp ground mixed spice
2 large egg whites
50 g/1¾ oz golden caster sugar
½ tsp freshly grated nutmeg
1 tsp gold dragées

For the Filling
55 g/2 oz unsalted butter,
  softened
juice and finely grated rind of
  ½ orange
1 tsp ground mixed spice
115 g/4 oz icing sugar, sifted
25 g/1 oz glacé cherries,
  finely chopped

Gingernuts

Makes 30

Ingredients

350 g/12 oz self-raising flour
pinch of salt
200 g/7 oz caster sugar
1 tbsp ground ginger
1 tsp bicarbonate of soda
125 g/4½ oz butter,
  plus extra for greasing
70 g/2¾ oz golden syrup
1 egg, beaten
1 tsp grated orange rind

1. Preheat the oven to 160°C/325°F/Gas Mark 3. Lightly grease several baking sheets.

2. Sift together the flour, salt, sugar, ginger and bicarbonate of soda into a large mixing bowl.

3. Heat the butter and golden syrup together in a saucepan over a very low heat until the butter has melted. Remove the pan from the heat and leave to cool slightly, then pour the contents onto the dry ingredients.

4. Add the egg and orange rind and mix thoroughly with a wooden spoon to form a dough. Using your hands, carefully shape the dough into 30 even-sized balls. Place the balls on the prepared baking sheets, spaced well apart, then flatten them slightly with your fingers.

5. Bake in the preheated oven for 15–20 minutes, then carefully transfer to a wire rack to cool completely.

Oatmeal Cookies

1. Preheat the oven to 180°C /350°F/Gas Mark 4 and grease a large baking sheet.

2. Cream the butter and sugar together in a large mixing bowl. Beat in the egg, water and vanilla extract until the mixture is smooth.

3. In a separate bowl, mix the oats, flour, salt and bicarbonate of soda. Gradually stir the oat mixture into the creamed mixture until thoroughly combined.

4. Place well-spaced tablespoonfuls of the mixture onto the prepared baking sheet. Bake in the preheated oven for 15 minutes, or until golden brown. Remove from the oven and cool on a wire rack.

Makes 15

Ingredients
175 g/6 oz butter or margarine,
  plus extra for greasing
275 g/9¾ oz demerara sugar
1 egg
4 tbsp water
1 tsp vanilla extract
375 g/13 oz rolled oats
140 g/5 oz plain flour, sifted
1 tsp salt
½ tsp bicarbonate of soda

Jam Swirls

Makes 20

Ingredients

350 g/12 oz plain flour,
  plus extra for dusting
60 g/2¼ oz ground almonds
200 g/7 oz cold butter,
  cut into small dice
100 g/3½ oz caster sugar
grated rind of a small orange
pinch of salt
2 eggs, lightly beaten
1 egg yolk
1 tsp vanilla extract
200 g/7 oz cherry or
  raspberry jam
icing sugar, for dusting

1. Sift the flour onto a work surface and scatter the ground almonds on top, together with the diced butter. Sprinkle over the caster sugar, orange rind and salt and mix well. Add the eggs, egg yolk and vanilla extract and knead together to form a smooth dough. Wrap with clingfilm and rest in the refrigerator for at least an hour.

2. Preheat the oven to 180°C/350°F/Gas Mark 4. Line a baking sheet with baking paper.

3. Turn the dough out onto a floured surface and roll it out to a thickness of 2–3 mm/⅛ inch. Brush the excess flour away and use three pastry cutters with 6-cm/2½-inch, 4.5-cm/1¾-inch and 3-cm/1¼-inch diameters to cut out biscuits. Use a 1-cm/½-inch diameter cutter to cut out the centre and create a ring from the smallest biscuit. Place on the prepared baking tray lined with baking paper.

4. Bake in the preheated oven for about 12 minutes. Remove the rings after 8 minutes as they will brown faster than the other biscuits.

5. While the biscuits are cooling, gently warm the jam and pass through a fine sieve. Spread the jam on the biscuits and build the jam swirls up, finishing with the rings. Finally, dust with the icing sugar to serve.

Reindeer Cookies

1. Crush the cardamom pods lightly in a pestle and mortar and discard the shells. Grind the cardamom seeds to a powder. Beat together the butter and caster sugar in a bowl with a whisk until creamy, then gradually beat in the egg, orange rind and cardamom powder.

2. Sift together the flour, cornflour and baking powder into the mixture and stir with a wooden spoon to form a soft dough. Wrap the dough in clingfilm and chill in the refrigerator for 30 minutes.

3. Preheat the oven to 180°C/350°F/Gas Mark 4. Grease three baking sheets. Roll out the chilled dough on a lightly floured work surface to 3 mm/⅛ inch thick. Cut out shapes using a reindeer-shaped cutter, and place on the prepared baking sheets. Re-knead and re-roll trimmings and cut out more shapes until all the dough is used up.

4. Bake in the preheated oven for 15 minutes, until just golden. Allow to cool for 5 minutes before transferring to a wire rack to cool completely.

5. Mix together the icing sugar and lemon juice until smooth. Spoon 2 tablespoons of the mixture into a separate mixing bowl and colour it with the red food colouring. Spoon the rest of the icing into a piping bag fitted with a fine nozzle and pipe antlers, hooves, tail, collar and a saddle in white icing on the cookies. Pipe a nose using the red icing. For the eye, fix a silver ball using a blob of icing.

Makes 25

Ingredients
10 cardamom pods
100 g/3½ oz butter, softened,
  plus extra for greasing
55 g/2 oz caster sugar
1 egg, beaten
finely grated rind of ½ orange
225 g/8 oz plain flour,
  plus extra for dusting
25 g/1 oz cornflour
½ tsp baking powder

For the Decoration
90 g/3¼ oz icing sugar
4 tsp lemon juice
glycerine-based red food
  colouring
25 edible silver balls

Sticky Ginger Cookies

Makes 20

Ingredients
225 g/8 oz butter, softened
140 g/5 oz golden caster sugar
1 egg yolk, lightly beaten
55 g/2 oz stem ginger, roughly
   chopped, plus 1 tbsp syrup
   from the jar
280 g/10 oz plain flour
pinch of salt
55 g/2 oz plain chocolate chips

1. Put the butter and sugar into a bowl and mix well with a wooden spoon, then beat in the egg yolk and ginger syrup. Sift together the flour and a pinch of salt into the mixture, add the stem ginger and chocolate chips and stir until thoroughly combined.

2. Shape the mixture into a log, wrap in clingfilm and chill in the refrigerator for 30–60 minutes.

3. Preheat the oven to 190°C/375°F/Gas Mark 5. Line two baking sheets with baking paper.

4. Unwrap the log and cut it into 5-mm/¼-inch slices with a sharp serrated knife. Put them on the prepared baking sheets, spaced well apart.

5. Bake in the preheated oven for 12–15 minutes, until golden brown. Leave to cool on the baking sheets for 5–10 minutes, then, using a palette knife, carefully transfer the cookies to wire racks to cool completely.

Chequerboard Cookies

1. Put the butter and sugar into a bowl and mix well with a wooden spoon, then beat in the egg yolk and vanilla extract. Sift together the flour and salt into the mixture and stir until thoroughly combined.

2. Divide the dough in half. Add the ginger and orange rind to one half and mix well. Shape the dough into a log 15 cm/ 6 inches long. Flatten the sides and top to square off the log to 5 cm/2 inches high. Wrap in clingfilm and chill in the refrigerator for 30–60 minutes. Add the cocoa to the other half of the dough and mix well. Shape into a flattened log exactly the same size as the first one, wrap in clingfilm and chill in the refrigerator for 30–60 minutes.

3. Unwrap the dough and cut each flattened log horizontally into three slices. Cut each slice lengthways into three strips. Brush the strips with egg white and stack them in threes, alternating the colours, so they are the same shape as the original logs. Wrap in clingfilm and chill in the refrigerator for 30–60 minutes. Preheat the oven to 190°C/375°F/Gas Mark 5. Line two baking sheets with baking paper.

4. Unwrap the logs and cut into slices with a sharp serrated knife. Put the cookies on the prepared baking sheets, spaced well apart. Bake in the preheated oven for 12–15 minutes, until firm. Leave to cool for 5–10 minutes, then carefully transfer to wire racks to cool completely.

Makes 20

Ingredients
225 g/8 oz butter, softened
140 g/5 oz caster sugar
1 egg yolk, lightly beaten
2 tsp vanilla extract
280 g/10 oz plain flour
pinch of salt
1 tsp ground ginger
1 tbsp finely grated orange rind
1 tbsp cocoa powder, sifted
1 egg white, lightly beaten

Viennese Fingers

Makes about 16

Ingredients
100 g/3½ oz unsalted butter,
  plus extra for greasing
25 g/1 oz golden caster sugar
½ tsp vanilla extract
100 g/3½ oz self-raising flour
100 g/3½ oz plain chocolate

1. Preheat the oven to 160°C/325°F/Gas Mark 3. Lightly grease two baking sheets.

2. Place the butter, sugar and vanilla extract in a bowl and cream together until pale and fluffy. Stir in the flour, mixing evenly to a fairly stiff dough.

3. Place the mixture in a piping bag fitted with a large star nozzle and pipe about 16 fingers, each 6 cm/2½ inches long, onto the prepared baking sheets.

4. Bake in the preheated oven for 10–15 minutes, until pale golden. Cool for 2–3 minutes on the baking sheets, then lift carefully onto a wire rack with a palette knife to cool completely.

5. Place the chocolate in a small heatproof bowl set over a pan of gently simmering water until melted. Remove from the heat. Dip the ends of each biscuit into the chocolate to coat, then place on a sheet of baking paper and leave to set.

Almond Macaroons

1. Preheat the oven to 180°C/350°F/Gas Mark 4. Line two baking sheets with baking paper.

2. Beat the egg white with a fork until frothy, then stir in the ground almonds, sugar and almond extract, mixing to form a sticky dough.

3. Using lightly sugared hands, roll the dough into small balls and place on the prepared baking sheets. Press an almond half into the centre of each.

4. Bake in the preheated oven for 15–20 minutes, or until pale golden. Place on a wire rack to cool.

Makes 12–14

Ingredients
1 egg white
85 g/3 oz ground almonds
85 g/3 oz caster sugar,
  plus extra for rolling
½ tsp almond extract
6–7 blanched almonds,
  split in half

Gift Cookies

Makes 30

Ingredients
225 g/8 oz butter, softened
140 g/5 oz caster sugar
1 egg yolk, lightly beaten
2 tsp orange juice or
  orange liqueur
finely grated rind of
  1 orange
280 g/10 oz plain flour
pinch of salt

For the Decoration
1 egg white
225 g/8 oz icing sugar
few drops each of 2 food
  colourings
edible silver balls

1. Place the butter and caster sugar in a large bowl and beat together until pale and creamy, then beat in the egg yolk, orange juice and grated rind. Sift together the flour and salt into the mixture and stir until combined. Halve the dough, shape into balls, wrap in clingfilm and chill in the refrigerator for 30–60 minutes.

2. Preheat the oven to 190°C/375°F/Gas Mark 5. Line two large baking sheets with baking paper. Unwrap the dough and roll out to 3 mm/⅛ inch thick. Cut out star and holly shapes with cookie cutters and place them on the prepared baking sheets, spaced well apart. Bake in the preheated oven for 10–15 minutes, or until light golden brown.

3. Leave to cool on the baking sheets for 5–10 minutes, then transfer to wire racks to cool completely.

4. Leave the cookies on the racks. Put the egg white and icing sugar into a bowl and beat until smooth, adding a little water if necessary. Transfer half the icing to another bowl and colour each bowl with a different colour. Put both icings in piping bags with fine nozzles and use to decorate the cookies and write the initials of the person who will receive the cookies as a gift. Finish with silver balls and leave to set.

Index